THE
COMFORT
BOOK

ALSO BY MATT HAIG

The Last Family in England
The Dead Fathers Club
The Possession of Mr Cave
The Radleys
The Humans
Humans: An A–Z
Reasons to Stay Alive
How to Stop Time
Notes on a Nervous Planet
The Midnight Library

For Children
The Runaway Troll
Shadow Forest
To Be A Cat
Echo Boy
A Boy Called Christmas
The Girl Who Saved Christmas
Father Christmas and Me
The Truth Pixie
Evie and the Animals
The Truth Pixie Goes to School
Evie in the Jungle

THE
COMFORT
BOOK

Matt Haig

CANONGATE

First published in Great Britain in 2021
by Canongate Books Ltd, 14 High Street, Edinburgh EH1 1TE

canongate.co.uk

2

For permission credits please see p. 259–60

British Library Cataloguing-in-Publication Data
A catalogue record for this book is available on
request from the British Library

ISBN 978 1 78689 829 6
Export ISBN: 978 1 83885 393 8

Typeset in Baskerville by
Palimpsest Book Production Ltd, Falkirk, Stirlingshire

Printed and bound in Great Britain by Clays Ltd, Elcograf S.p.A.

Do not think that the person who is trying to
console you lives effortlessly among the simple,
quiet words that sometimes make you feel better . . .
But if it were any different he could never
have found the words that he did.

Rainer Maria Rilke, *Letters to a Young Poet*

Introduction

I sometimes write things down to comfort myself. Stuff learned in the bad times. Thoughts. Meditations. Lists. Examples. Things I want to remind myself of. Or things I have learned from other people or other lives.

It is a strange paradox, that many of the clearest, most comforting life lessons are learned while we are at our lowest. But then we never think about food more than when we are hungry and we never think about life rafts more than when we are thrown overboard.

So, these are some of my life rafts. The thoughts that have kept me afloat. I hope some of them might carry you to dry land too.

A note on structure

This book is as messy as life.

It has a lot of short chapters and some longer ones. It contains lists and aphorisms and quotes and case studies and more lists and even the occasional recipe. It is influenced by experience but has moments of inspiration taken from anything ranging from quantum physics to philosophy, from movies I like to ancient religions to Instagram.

You can read it how you want. You can start at the beginning and end at the end, or you can start at the end and end at the beginning, or you can just dip into it.

You can crease the pages. You can tear out the pages. You can lend it to a friend (though maybe not if you've torn out the pages). You can place it beside your bed or keep it next to the toilet. You can throw it out of the window. There are no rules.

There is a kind of accidental theme, though. The theme

is connection. We are all things. And we connect to all things. Human to human. Moment to moment. Pain to pleasure. Despair to hope.

When times are hard, we need a deep kind of comfort. Something elemental. A solid support. A rock to hold on to.

The kind we already have inside us. But which we sometimes need a bit of help to see.

PART ONE

Perhaps home is not a place
but simply an irrevocable condition.

James Baldwin, *Giovanni's Room*

Baby

Imagine yourself as a baby. You would look at that baby and think they lacked nothing. That baby came complete. Their value was innate from their first breath. Their value did not depend on external things like wealth or appearance or politics or popularity. It was the infinite value of a human life. And that value stays with us, even as it becomes easier to forget it. We stay precisely as alive and precisely as human as we were the day we were born. The only thing we need is to exist. And to hope.

You are the goal

You don't have to continually improve yourself to love yourself. Love is not something you only deserve if you reach a goal. The world is one of pressure but don't let it squeeze your self-compassion. You were born worthy of love and you remain worthy of love. Be kind to yourself.

Nothing is stronger than a small hope that doesn't give up.

A thing my dad said once
when we were lost in a forest

Once upon a time, my father and I got lost in a forest in France. I must have been about twelve or thirteen. Anyway, it was before the era when most people owned a mobile phone. We were on holiday, the rural, landlocked, basic kind of middle-class holiday I didn't really understand. It was in the Loire Valley, and we had gone for a run. About half an hour in, my dad realised the truth. 'Oh, it seems that we're lost.' We walked round and round in circles, trying to find the path, but with no luck. My dad asked two men – poachers – for directions and they sent us the wrong way. I could tell my dad was starting to panic, even as he was trying to hide it from me. We had been in the forest for hours now and both knew my mum would be in a state of absolute terror. At school, I had just been told the Bible story of the Israelites who had died in the wilderness and I found it easy to imagine that would be our fate too. 'If we keep going in a straight line we'll get out of here,' my dad said.

And he was right. Eventually we heard the sound of cars and reached a main road. We were eleven miles from the village where we had started off, but at least we had signposts now. We were clear of the trees. And I often think of that strategy, when I am totally lost – literally or metaphorically. I thought of it when I was in the middle of a breakdown. When I was living in a panic attack punctuated only by depression, when my heart pounded rapidly with fear, when I hardly knew who I was and didn't know how I could carry on living. *If we keep going in a straight line we'll get out of here.* Walking one foot in front of the other, in the same direction, will always get you further than running around in circles. It's about the determination to keep walking forward.

It's okay

It's okay to be broken.

It's okay to wear the scars of experience.

It's okay to be a mess.

It's okay to be the teacup with a chip in it. That's the one with a story.

It's okay to be sentimental and whimsical and cry bittersweet tears at songs and movies you aren't supposed to love.

It's okay to like what you like.

It's okay to like things for literally no other reason than because you like them and not because they are cool or clever or popular.

It's okay to let people find you. You don't have to spread yourself so thin you become invisible. You don't have to always be the person reaching out. You can sometimes allow yourself to be reached. As the great writer Anne Lamott puts it: 'Lighthouses don't go running all over an island for boats to save; they just stand there shining.'

It's okay not to make the most of every chunk of time.

It's okay to be who you are.

It's okay.

Power

Marcus Aurelius, Roman emperor and Stoic philosopher, thought that if we are distressed about something external, 'the pain is not due to the thing itself, but to your estimate of it; and this you have the power to revoke at any moment'.

I love this, but also know from experience that finding that power can be near impossible at times. We can't just click our fingers and be rid of, say, grief, or the stress of work, or health worries. When we are lost in the forest, our fear might not be directly caused by the forest, or our being lost in said forest, but while we are actively lost in the forest it very much feels like the source of our fear is *being lost in the forest.*

But it is helpful to remember that our perspective *is* our world. And our external circumstances don't need to change in order for our perspective to change. And the forests we find ourselves in are metaphorical, and sometimes we are unable to escape them, but with a change of perspective we can live among the trees.

Nothing either good or bad

When Hamlet tells his old university buddies Rosencrantz and Guildenstern that 'there is nothing either good or bad, but thinking makes it so', he doesn't mean this in a positive way. Shakespeare's prince is in a foul and depressed mood, but with reason. He is talking about Denmark, and indeed the whole world, being a prison. For him, Denmark really is a physical and psychological prison. But he is also aware that perspective plays a part in this. And that the world and Denmark aren't *intrinsically* bad. They are bad from his *perspective*. They are bad because he thinks they are.

External events are neutral. They only gain positive or negative value the moment they enter our minds. It is ultimately up to us how we greet these things. It's not always easy, sure, but there is a comfort in knowing it is possible to view any single thing in multiple ways. It also empowers us, because we aren't at the mercy of the world we can never control, we are at the mercy of a mind we can, potentially, with effort and determination, begin to alter and expand. Our mind might make prisons, but it also gives us keys.

Change is real

We turn keys all the time. Or rather: time turns keys all the time. Because time means change.

And change is the nature of life. The reason to hope.

Neuroplasticity is the way our brains change their structure according to the things we experience. None of us are the same people we were ten years ago. When we feel or experience terrible things, it is useful to remember that nothing lasts. Perspective shifts. We become different versions of ourselves. The hardest question I have ever been asked is: 'How do I stay alive for other people if I have no one?' The answer is that you stay alive for other versions of you. For the people you will *meet*, yes, sure, but also the people you will *be*.

To be is to let go

Self-forgiveness makes the world better. You don't become a good person by believing you are a bad one.

Somewhere

Hope is a beautiful thing to find in art or stories or music. It is often a surprise moment, like in *The Shawshank Redemption* when the poster of Raquel Welch is pulled off the wall in Andy's prison cell. Or in *The Sound of Music* when Captain von Trapp switches from repressed widower to singing father in the space of a single scene.

It is often subtle, but you know it when you feel it. Like when 'Somewhere Over the Rainbow' effortlessly goes up a whole octave within the word 'somewhere', jumping clean over seven natural keys – an actual musical rainbow – before landing on the eighth. Hope always involves a soaring and a reaching. Hope flies. The thing with feathers, as Emily Dickinson said.

People often imagine it is hard to feel hopeful when times are tough, yet I tend to think the opposite. Or at least, hope is the thing we most want to cling on to in periods of despair or worry. I think that it's no coincidence that 'Somewhere Over the Rainbow', one of the most bittersweet yet hopeful songs in the world, a song that has topped polls as the greatest song of the twentieth century, was written by Harold Arlen and Yip Harburg for *The Wizard of Oz* in one of the bleakest years in human history: 1939. Harold wrote the music, while Yip penned the words. Harold and Yip themselves were no strangers to suffering. Yip had seen the horrors of the First World War and was left bankrupt following the crash of 1929. As for Harold, who would become known for his hopeful octave-leaping, he was born with a twin brother who sadly died in infancy. Aged sixteen, Harold fled his Jewish Orthodox parents and pursued a modern musical path. And let's not forget these were two Jewish musicians writing arguably the most hopeful song ever written, all while Adolf Hitler was triggering war and anti-semitism was on the rise.

To feel hope you don't need to be in a great situation. You just need to understand that things will change. Hope is available to all. You don't need to deny the reality of the present in order to have hope, you just need to know the future is uncertain, and that life contains light as well as dark. We can have our feet right here where we are, while our minds can hear another octave, right over the rainbow. We can be half inside the present, half inside the future. Half in Kansas, half in Oz.

Songs that comfort me – a playlist

(These aren't all comforting lyrically, or comforting in a logical way, but they all comfort me through the direct or indirect magic only music can muster. You will have different ones. But I thought I'd share some of mine.)

O-o-h Child – The Five Stairsteps
Here Comes the Sun – The Beatles
Dear Theodosia – *Hamilton* soundtrack
Don't Worry Baby – The Beach Boys
Somewhere Over the Rainbow – Judy Garland
A Change Is Gonna Come – Sam Cooke
The People – Common ft. Dwele
The Boys of Summer – Don Henley
California – Joni Mitchell
Secret Garden – Bruce Springsteen
You Make It Easy – Air

These Dreams – Heart

True Faith – New Order

If You Leave – OMD

Ivy – Frank Ocean

Swim Good – Frank Ocean

Steppin' Out – Joe Jackson

'Pas de deux' from *The Nutcracker* – Tchaikovsky (not a song, obviously, but an epic bittersweet comfort)

If I Could Change Your Mind – HAIM

Space Cowboy – Kacey Musgraves

Hounds of Love – either the Kate Bush or Futureheads version

Enjoy the Silence – Depeche Mode

I Won't Let You Down – Ph.D.

Just Like Heaven – The Cure

Promised Land – Joe Smooth

Mountain

In order to get over a problem it helps to look at it. You can't climb a mountain that you pretend isn't there.

Valley

When you feel low, it is important to bear in mind that thoughts inspired by those feelings are not external, objective facts. For instance, when I was twenty-four I was convinced I would never see my twenty-fifth birthday. I knew for certain that I wouldn't be able to survive for weeks or months with the mental pain I was suddenly encountering. And yet here I am, aged forty-five, writing this paragraph. Depression lies. And while the feelings themselves were real, the things they led me to believe were resolutely not.

Because I didn't really understand how I fell into suicidal depression, I imagined I would never find my way out. I didn't realise that there is something bigger than depression, and that thing is time. Time disproves the lies depression tells. Time showed me that the things depression imagined for me were fallacies, not prophecies.

That doesn't mean time dissolves all mental health issues.

But it does mean our attitudes and approaches to our own mind change and often improve via sticking around long enough to gain the perspective despair and fear refuse to give.

People talk of peaks and troughs in relation to mental health. Hills and valleys. And such topographical metaphors make sense. You can definitely feel the steep descents and uphill struggles in life. But it is important to remember the bottom of the valley never has the clearest view. And that sometimes all you need to do in order to rise up again is to keep moving forward.

Sum

We are always bigger than the pain we feel. Always. The pain is not total. When you say 'I am in pain', there is the pain and there is the I but the I is always bigger than the pain. Because the I is there even without the pain, while the pain is only there as a product of that I. And that I will survive and go on to feel other things.

I used to struggle with understanding this. I used to think I *was* the pain. I didn't always think of depression as an experience. I thought of it as something I was. Even as I walked away from a cliff-edge in Spain. Even as I flew back to my parents' house and told my loved ones I was going to be okay. I called myself a depressive. I rarely said 'I have depression' or 'I am currently experiencing depression' because I imagined the depression was the sum of who I was. I was mistaking the film on the screen with the cinema itself. I thought there would only ever be one film playing for all eternity, on rotation. *A Nightmare on Haig Street*. (Sorry.) I didn't realise there would one day be showings of *The Sound of Music* and *It's a Wonderful Life*.

The trouble was that I had a very binary view of things. I thought you were either well or ill, sane or insane, and once I was diagnosed with depression I felt I had been exiled to a new land, like Napoleon, and that there would be no escape back to the world I had known.

And in one sense I was right. I never really went back. I went forward. Because that is what happens, whether we try for it or not, we move forward, through time, simply by staying alive. And slowly our experiences change. I, for instance, discovered little moments of happiness or humour within despair. I realised things weren't always one thing or another thing. They were sometimes both.

And as soon as we notice all that space inside us, we have a new perspective. Yes, there is room for a lot of pain, but there is room for other things too. And indeed, pain might be a total arsehole, but it can inadvertently show us how much space we have inside. It can even expand that space. And enable us to experience the equivalent quantity of joy or hope or love or contentment at some future point in time.

So, in other words, it is important to always realise our own vastness. Our own rooms. We are multiplexes of possibility.

The subject in the sentence

And yes, we might feel that others are judging our worth via metrics like income and follower counts and weight and chest measurements and all the rest of it, but always remember we are more than can be measured. We are life itself. We aren't the narrow band of feelings in a single moment. We are the vessel that could contain *any* feeling. We are the subject in the sentence. We are more than the sum of our achievements. We are more than the feelings we witness. We are the infinity that remains when you subtract them.

To remember during the bad days

It won't last.

You have felt other things. You will feel other things again.

Emotions are like weather. They change and shift. Clouds can seem as still as stone. We look at them and hardly notice a change at all. And yet they always move.

The worst part of any experience is the part where you feel like you can't take it any more. So, if you feel like you can't take it any more, the chances are you are already at the worst point. The only feelings you have left to experience are better than this one.

You are still here. And that is everything.

For when you reach rock bottom

You have survived everything you have been through, and you will survive this too. Stay for the person you will become. You are more than a bad day, or week, or month, or year, or even decade. You are a future of multifarious possibility. You are another self at a point in future time looking back in gratitude that this lost and former you held on. Stay.

Rock

The best thing about rock bottom is the rock part. You discover the solid bit of you. The bit that can't be broken down further. The thing that you might sentimentally call a soul. At our lowest we find the solid ground of our foundation. And we can build ourselves anew.

Ten books that helped my mind

1. *Letters to a Young Poet* – Rainer Maria Rilke
2. *Poems* – Emily Dickinson
3. Henry David Thoreau's journal
4. *When Things Fall Apart* – Pema Chödrön
5. *The House at Pooh Corner* – A.A. Milne
6. *Bird by Bird* – Anne Lamott
7. *Meditations* – Marcus Aurelius
8. *Tao Te Ching* – Laozi
9. *Serious Concerns* – Wendy Cope
10. *Dream Work* – Mary Oliver

Words

At university, doing my master's degree in English Literature, I continually felt stupid, and the reason for this was that I had chosen a module called 'Critical Theory'. This involved reading a lot of French postmodern and post-structuralist philosophy, which even when translated into English contained so many apparently deliberately and playfully obscure sentences that I had to stare at each one for about half an hour to even begin to fathom it. In particular I studied just enough to know that there is always a gap between the signifier and the signified. The word 'dog' is not a dog. The word 'water' is not water. A painting of a pipe is not a pipe. TV footage of a war is not a war. On the whole, these theories came across as really complicated and obtuse ways to state the depressingly obvious: we are always grasping after a meaning we can never quite reach.

But when I became ill, they took on a broader meaning.

I felt like a walking signifier, signifying a person I could never quite be. There was a gap between what I looked like and what I felt like. And the only way to bridge that gap was by talking and writing about what was going on inside me. And yes, in the philosophical sense, words are never quite the thing they describe, but that is also their use. They can help externalise internal things. The moment we try and turn a thought into words we place it into a shared world. This shared world we call 'language'. Once we take our personal unseen experiences and make them seen, we help others, and even ourselves, to understand what we are going through. What we say aloud can never quite capture what we feel inside, but that is almost the point.

Words don't capture, they release.

Words (two)

So, yes.

Words are important.

Words can hurt. Words can heal. Words can comfort.

There was a time when I couldn't speak.

There was a time when my depression was so heavy my tongue wouldn't move. A time when the distance between the open gate of my mouth and the storm of my mind seemed too far.

I could manage monosyllables, sometimes.

I could nod. I could mumble. But I sounded as if I were in slow motion. Underwater.

I was lost.

To want to speak was to want to live. And in those depths I wanted neither. I just wanted to want, if that makes sense.

I remembered reading Maya Angelou's *I Know Why the Caged Bird Sings* at school. I remember reading about how, as a child, she had stopped talking for five years after suffering the most horrific sexual abuse at the hands of her mother's boyfriend, Mr Freeman. When the man was killed by her uncles, eight-year-old Maya felt such guilt for his death that she stopped talking, becoming effectively mute for years. It was through a family friend and teacher, Bertha Flowers, that Maya was exposed to great writers. She read Edgar Allan Poe and Charles Dickens and Shakespeare and the poets Georgia Douglas Johnson and Frances Harper. Slowly, through reading and learning, Maya found her voice again, and never let it go. By the late 1960s this mute girl had become one of the key voices of the civil rights movement. A voice that not only spoke for herself, but for millions of people facing racial discrimination.

Language gives us the power to voice our experience, to reconnect with the world, and to change our own and other people's lives.

'There is no greater agony than bearing an untold story inside you', wrote Angelou. Silence is pain. But it is a pain with an exit route. When we can't speak, we can write. When we can't write, we can read. When we can't read, we can listen. Words are seeds. Language is a way back to life. And it is sometimes the most vital comfort we have.

The power of why

One thing I have been asked a few times is this: 'Does writing about bad experiences make you feel worse?'

I understand why people ask the question, but for me the answer is a profound 'No'.

I discovered this years ago. When I was very ill, at the lowest of the low, when I could hardly speak, I wrote down what I was feeling. One day I wrote down the words 'invisible weight'. Another day I wrote 'I wish I could claw into my head and take out the part of my brain that makes me feel like this'. There were even darker things I put down. But writing down darkness didn't make me feel dark. I already felt dark. Writing things down brought that inner darkness into external light.

Nowadays, I sometimes write about what I want. The key to this is honesty. Be brutally, humiliatingly honest. I recommend this.

For instance, you could write 'I want a six-pack'.

And seeing that wish on the page might automatically make you realise something about it. It might make you feel silly for having it. You might already be awakening another part of you that helps you diminish the craving. But either way, it is good to ask a single-word question after it. 'Why?' *Why do I want a six-pack?* Then to be entirely honest in your answer. 'I want to look good.' And again: 'Why?' 'For myself.' And then you might stare at that answer for a while and feel you weren't being entirely honest. So you add: 'To impress other people.' And then, like some incessant Socrates, ask it again: 'Why?' 'Because I want their approval.' 'Why?' 'Because I want to belong.' 'Why?' And you can keep going, deeper and deeper, through the tunnel of whys, until you reach the light of realisation. And the realisation may be that wanting the six-pack wasn't really about the six-pack. It wasn't about your body. It wasn't even about health or strength or fitness. It was about something else entirely. Something that wouldn't be fundamentally addressed or solved by gaining the six-pack.

Writing, then, is a kind of seeing. A way to see your insecurities more clearly. A way to shine a light on doubts and dreams and realise what they are actually about. It can dissolve a whole puddle of worries in the bright light of truth.

The gaps of life

If you take objects out of a room, one by one, two things will happen. The first is obvious. You will miss some of the things you have taken away. The second is that you will notice the things that remain more than ever. Your attention will focus. You will be more likely to read the books that are left on the shelves. You will appreciate the remaining chairs more. And if there is a chess board, you are more likely to play chess. When things are taken from us, the stuff that remains has more value. It rises not only in visibility but also intensity. What we lose in breadth we gain in depth.

A few don'ts

Don't envy things you wouldn't actually want.

Don't absorb criticism from people you wouldn't go to for advice.

Don't fear missing parties you would probably want to leave.

Don't worry about fitting in. Be your own tribe.

Don't argue with people who will never understand you.

Don't believe anyone has it all figured out.

Don't imagine there is an amount of money or success or fame that could insulate you from pain.

Don't think there is a type of face or job or relationship that safeguards happiness.

Don't say yes to things you wish you had the confidence to say no to.

Don't worry if you do.

Foundation

Other people matter. But there is no point becoming someone else in order to find friends. In order to find the people who like you, it is first necessary to *be* you.

Purple saxifrage

The hardiest plant in the world is the purple saxifrage. It has delicate-looking flowers, with purple petals that seem as though they might blow away in the wind, yet it thrives in the Arctic. The flowers survive by clustering together, low to the ground, offering each other shelter against the hardest conditions on earth.

Connected

We all have an impact on each other. We are all connected in so many seen and unseen ways. Which possibly explains why one of the simplest and quickest routes to happiness seems to be to make someone else happy. The reason to be selfless is selfish. Nothing makes ourselves feel better than not thinking of our *selves*.

A thing I discovered recently

I love stillness. Slowness. When nothing is happening. The blueness of the sky. Inhaling clear air. Birdsong over traffic. Lone footsteps. Spring flowers blooming with defiance. I used to think the quiet patches felt dead. Now they feel more alive. Like leaning over and listening to the earth's heartbeat.

Pear

Forward momentum is great. But we also need sideways momentum. For instance, I just sat down and ate a pear. I have no idea what the future holds but I am very grateful that I am alive and able to sit on a sofa and eat a pear.

Toast

Continually looking for the meaning of life is like looking for the meaning of toast. It is sometimes better just to eat the toast.

Hummus

Cooking can be therapeutic. But personally I find the most therapeutic kind of cooking to be the kind where there is no actual *cooking*. Where the recipe is so simple it is just a case of bringing all the ingredients together and mixing them up. A kind of get-together for food. A literal mash-up. And the thing I enjoy non-cooking the most is hummus. Hummus is in and of itself a comforting food, which is probably why – when it eventually got noticed beyond the Middle East – it took off very quickly. I don't know what it is about hummus that is so comforting. Yotam Ottolenghi talks of the 'emotive power' of hummus and how, within the Middle East, it sparks serious rivalries. It feels, somehow, *more* than a food. It is the default dip. Culinary oxygen. I struggle to imagine a world without it. Well, I can. But it would be a slightly sadder world. I have been making my own variants for years but only recently hit upon my favourite formula.

As for ingredients, take two tins of chickpeas, a massive scoop of tahini, garlic (quantity-wise err on the side of incaution), a few glugs of olive oil, the juice of one lemon, some water for texture, and a generous sprinkle each of cumin, cayenne and salt. Blend the lot. Serve with more cumin and oil. Take some bread, preferably warm and fresh. An olive roll, pitta, whatever. Tear, and dunk, and enjoy.

There is always a path through the forest

I've spent much of my life thinking about hope. In recent years I've spent a lot of time writing about it. Before then, I clutched hope like a security blanket. In my twenties I had a breakdown. A fusion of severe depression and panic disorder that made me fall so hard I spent three years of my life desperately wanting to die. It is hard to cultivate hope in such a state of despair, but, somehow, I gathered enough of it to stay alive and see a better future.

Hope can feel in scarce supply for everyone these days. Global pandemics, brutal injustices, political turmoil and glaring inequalities can all take their toll on your reserves. And yet, the thing with hope is that it is persistent. It has the potential to exist even in the most troubled times.

Hope isn't the same thing as happiness. You don't need to be happy to be hopeful. You need instead to accept the unknowability of the future, and that there are versions of that future which could be better than the present. Hope, in its simplest form, is the acceptance of possibility.

The acceptance that if we are suddenly lost in a forest, there will be a way through.

All we need is a plan, and a little determination.

Pizza

The sky isn't more beautiful if you have perfect skin. Music doesn't sound more interesting if you have a six-pack. Dogs aren't better company if you're famous. Pizza tastes good regardless of your job title. The best of life exists beyond the things we are encouraged to crave.

A little plan

Be curious. Go outside. Get to bed on time. Hydrate. Breathe from the diaphragm. Eat happy. Get a routine baggy enough to live in. Be kind. Accept that not everyone will like you. Appreciate those who do. Don't be defined. Allow fuck-ups. Want what you already have. Learn to say no to things that get in the way of life. And to say yes to the things that help you live.

Ladders

We are often encouraged to see life as one continual uphill climb. We talk about ladders without even thinking. Career ladders. Property ladders. Of being on the top rung of the ladder. Or the bottom rung of the ladder. We talk of climbing the ladder. We talk of rising up. We talk of uphill struggles. In doing so we visualise life as a kind of vertical race, like we are human skyscrapers reaching for the clouds. And we risk only ever looking above to the future or below to the past and never around at the infinite horizontal landscape of the present. The trouble with ladders is they give you no room to move around. Just room to fall.

Life is not

a ladder to climb
a puzzle to solve
a key to find
a destination to reach
a problem to fix

Life is

'understood backwards; but it must be lived forwards'

(Søren Kierkegaard)

My formula for greatness in a human being is *amor fati*: that one wants nothing to be different, not forward, not backward, not in all eternity. Not merely bear what is necessary, still less conceal it . . . but love it.

Friedrich Nietzsche

Chapter

There is no point spending an entire life trying to win the love you didn't feel when you needed it. You sometimes just have to let go of an old story and start your own. Give yourself some love. You can't change the past. You can't change other people. You can change you though. You narrate this story. So start to write a new chapter.

Room

Imagine forgiving yourself completely. The goals you didn't reach. The mistakes you made. Instead of locking those flaws inside to define and repeat yourself, imagine letting your past float through your present and away like air through a window, freshening a room. Imagine that.

No

No.

No, I don't want to.

No, I don't want to write that article for free.

No, I am not on for Tuesday.

No, I don't want another drink.

No, I don't agree with you on that actually.

No, I can't always snap out of it.

No, I wasn't rude when I didn't get back to a message I
never saw.

No, if it's okay I don't want to collaborate with you.

No, I am not dumbing down.

No, I can't do any dates in July.

No, I don't want your leaflet.

No, I don't want to continue watching.

No, my niceness is not weakness.

No, they aren't the next Beatles.

No, I'm not going to take that crap.

No, my masculinity does not mean I shouldn't cry.

No, I don't need to buy what you are selling.

No, I am not ashamed to make time for myself.

No, I am not going to your school reunion when you never spoke to me at school.

No, I will no longer apologise for being myself.

No.

No is a good word. It keeps you sane. In an age of overload, no is really yes. It is yes to having the space you need to live.

Be humble because you are made of earth.
Be noble, for you are made of stars.

Serbian proverb

The maze

It is rare to escape a maze on the first attempt. And when we are stuck in a maze, we can't escape by following the same path that got us lost. We escape a maze by trying new routes. We don't feel like we have failed when we hit a dead end. In fact, we appreciate the new knowledge. There is now a dead end we won't try any more. Every dead end and cul-de-sac helps us escape the maze. To know which path to take, it helps to take a few wrong ones.

Knowledge and the forest

'Know your enemy'. In the classic Chinese military treatise *The Art of War*, Sun Tzu offered advice that echoed through the centuries.

It is timeless advice because of course it doesn't just apply to war. If we fully understand, say, depression, or a physical disease, or the nature of climate change, or injustice, it helps us combat these things. Without knowledge of our difficulties, we would be in trouble.

For instance, the average person plunged into the middle of the Amazon rainforest would probably struggle to survive, because they wouldn't understand all the threats they faced. But Juliane Koepcke wasn't an average person. She was a person with knowledge.

On Christmas Eve 1971, aged seventeen, somewhere over Peru, Koepcke fell through the sky strapped to her seat after lightning struck her plane. All 91 of the other people on board died, including her own mother, but she survived the fall and managed to get out of her seat once it had fallen through the jungle canopy.

Koepcke was in pain. She was in shock. She had a broken collar bone and deep cuts on her legs. She was also in a state of fear for her own life. At the sight of other dead bodies she felt 'paralysed by panic'. She grabbed some provisions she found amid the debris and tried to find her way to civilisation.

Koepcke knew a lot about the rainforest. Her parents were both zoologists. Before the crash, she had spent over a year living with them in a research station within the Peruvian rainforest. In her own words she knew that, armed with knowledge, it didn't have to be the 'green hell' people imagined.

So, for instance, she knew that snakes could be camou-flaged to look like dried leaves. She knew the sounds of various bird calls. She knew which signs to look for in order to find water and she ended up finding a creek. Her dad had also once told her that if you followed the flow of running water you would eventually find civilisation.

As described in her book *When I Fell From the Sky*, she passed vultures feeding on corpses. Snakes, mosquitoes and deadly spiders were a continual threat. One of her wounds became infested with maggots. She suffered from the heat of the sun. But all the time she was aided by knowledge.

She decided to walk as much as possible in the water

of the stream, in order to avoid snakes, spiders and the poisonous plants of the jungle floor. She stayed in the middle of the stream in order to avoid piranhas, which she knew mainly swam in shallow water. She knew this would mean she would probably encounter alligators, but she also knew that, unlike snakes, alligators rarely attacked humans.

On and on she walked, as her infested wound grew ever more painful. She had no food now. She felt weary and in a dream-like state. Yet she had a determination she believed was passed down from her father: '"When we have really resolved to achieve something," my father once said, "we succeed. We only have to want it, Juliane."'

She stayed on the lookout for jungle paths, found one, and then followed it. It led her to a deserted hut which had a litre of petrol outside. She had also been taught that in an emergency petrol can be a (painful) remedy for severely infected wounds, so she used it to dress her own injury.

Eventually, on the eleventh day, she heard human voices and the jungle-dwelling men who found her took her on a long boat trip back to civilisation. The day after her rescue she was reunited with her father.

Koepcke's story would eventually be the subject of the Werner Herzog-directed documentary *Wings of Hope*, Herzog himself having originally been an intended passenger on the ill-fated plane. Juliane graduated in biology and kept the family tradition of zoology alive, as she is currently the librarian at the Bavarian State Collection of Zoology in Munich.

Of course, it is unlikely we will find ourselves in the middle of the Amazon stranded after a plane crash. But when we find ourselves lost and stranded in the tangled forests of our own lives we can still get to know the territory. And face up to our wounds and be aware of the metaphorical snakes in the undergrowth, not hindered by ignorance or denial, but armed with self-awareness.

Minds and windows

Self-awareness can be hard. Your mind is not always to be trusted. It sometimes lies, or plays tricks, or doesn't give you the full picture. It can convince you that you are terrible.

A mind is real *as a mind* in the same way a window is real *as a window.* But that doesn't mean the view you see through the window is the full view. Sometimes the glass is dirty, or clouded, or rain-specked, and sometimes the view is obscured by a big lorry that has parked right in front of it. The window could also be entirely misleading. For instance, if your only view was through a red stained-glass window you might perceive the world to be as red and forbidding as a Martian desert. Even if there was nothing out there but lush green fields.

A paradox

A therapist once told me that the most common complaint he heard from his patients was the feeling that they didn't belong. The feeling of being an imposter, or of being outside things, of not fitting in. Of failing to connect easily with people. I found this as reassuring as it was paradoxical. That one of the most common feelings among people was the feeling of not fitting in *among people*. The comfort, then, is the weird truth that in one sense we have most in common with others when we feel awkward and alone. Isolation is as universal as it gets.

Crossroads

Sometimes when we have a decision to make, we feel we need to be fast. Indeed, the word 'decisive' is often used as a synonym of fast. But when we find ourselves at a cross-roads it is often better to stop, wait a while at the lights and check the map. After all, movement isn't progress if we are heading in the wrong direction.

Happiness

Happiness occurs when you forget who you're expected to be. And what you're expected to do. Happiness is an accident of self-acceptance. It's the warm breeze you feel when you open the door to who you are.

When one door of happiness closes, another opens; but often we look so long at the closed door that we do not see the one which has been opened for us.

Helen Keller, *We Bereaved*

One beautiful thing

Experience one beautiful thing a day. However small. However trivial. Read a poem. Play a favourite song. Laugh with a friend. Gaze at the sky just before the sun's final tumble towards night. Watch a classic movie. Eat a slice of lemon drizzle cake. Whatever. Just give yourself one simple reminder that the world is full of wonders. Even if we are at a point in life where we can't appreciate things, it sometimes helps to remember there are things in this world to enjoy, when we are ready.

Growth

We grow through hard times. Growth is change. And when everything is easy, we have no reason to change. The most painful moments in life expand us. And when the pain leaves, space remains. Space we can fill with life itself.

Pasta

No physical appearance is worth not eating pasta for.

How to be random

When I am in search of some evidence of the freak randomness of my existence, I think of the generations directly
above me. I think of my grandmother, on my father's side,
who studied art at Central Saint Martins in the 1930s. As
part of her course she had a year's placement at an art
college in Vienna. While there she witnessed Hitler's annexation of Austria into Nazi Germany in 1938. My grandmother
was Jewish. And almost immediately after the annexation
– the Anschluss – Jewish people were targeted. Paraded in
the street, made to clean graffiti, publicly humiliated. My
grandmother got out. She caught the very last train to
France she could find, and according to family legend was
only allowed on board after flirting with the Nazi guard at
the station. She was barely more than a teenager. Then,
directly because of this proximity to the terrors of Nazism,
when war broke out she decided to become a volunteer

nurse and fell in love with my grandfather after he suffered burn injuries during the Blitz.

They had three children. One was my father, who in the 1960s dropped out of Oxford University to study architecture in Sheffield. It was there he met my mother, who had dropped out of drama school in Bristol to go to teacher training college in South Yorkshire. My mother, who had been abandoned as a baby for reasons she still doesn't understand, grew up with her adoptive parents on a farm in Devon, hundreds of miles away from my father's childhood home in Sussex, their paths not crossing until they both entered Sheffield's Queen's Head pub one day in 1969.

This is not that remarkable a story. Or rather, it is equally as remarkable as everyone's origin story. We all come from randomness. We exist out of uncertainty. Out of near impossibility. And yet we exist. So, when you feel the odds are against you it is important to realise that they are never so against you as they were when you didn't exist. And there you are, we are, existing.

The future is open

You don't need to know the future to be hopeful. You just need to embrace the concept of possibility. To accept that the unknowability of the future is the key, and that there are versions of that future which are brighter and fairer than the present. The future is open.

Being, not doing

You don't need to exhaust yourself trying to *find* your own value. You are not an iPhone needing an upgrade. Your value is not a condition of productivity or exercise or body shape or something you lose via inactivity. Value is not a plate that needs to be continually spun. The value is there. It is intrinsic, innate. It is in the 'being' not the 'doing'.

Short

Life is short. Be kind.

Peanut butter on toast

You will need:

Two slices of bread

A jar of peanut butter

Method:

1. Place the slices of bread in a toaster.
2. Wait a minute or two. Remove the toasted bread from the toaster and transfer to a plate.
3. With a knife, spread the peanut butter generously onto one side of the toast. Spread the peanut butter with the knife always travelling in the same direction over the toast. I don't know why. It just feels better this way.
4. Don't rush it. Set the mood of appreciation by moving the knife at a steady, Tai Chi kind of pace. This moment should have the integrity of a religious ritual.

5. Take the plate of toast to your favourite seat. Sit. Compose yourself. Be fully aware of how wondrous it is to be sentient. To be aware you are not only alive as a human being, but as a human being about to eat some *peanut butter on toast.*
6. Close your eyes as you take the first bite. Let your worries float by, untethered from their hooks, as you appreciate this living moment of taste and pleasure.
7. If you really don't like peanut butter, this ritual of gratitude and attentiveness has also been proven to work with marmalade.

PART TWO

Empty your mind, be formless. Shapeless, like water. Now, you put water into a cup, it becomes the cup. You put water into a bottle, it becomes the bottle. You put it in a teapot, it becomes the teapot. Now, water can flow or it can crash. Be water, my friend.

Bruce Lee

River

People talk a lot about flow. Workflow. Musical flow. Yoga flow. Life flow. If we are stressed about something we might be advised to 'go with' the flow. What does this even mean? In *Siddhartha*, Hermann Hesse's novel about one man's spiritual discovery, he writes 'the river is every-where'. The story is indeed partly centred around a river. The central character, Siddhartha himself, aims to live his life near a river which provides him with spiritual inspiration. The voices in the river teach him acceptance and spirituality. On the edge of suicide, he falls into a deep sleep and is saved by the soothing voice of the river which helps him discover a spirituality he'd never known. Later, the river teaches him that time is an illusion and that all his problems and pains are part of a larger fellowship of nature. Individual events mean nothing *by themselves*, but are part of a larger totality and can only be understood within the whole. This is what the river teaches him.

For me, the flow of life is about accepting things as part of something bigger. Accepting every molecule of water as part of the river. This comforts me when I have moments of torment or suffering.

Pain is selfish. It demands full attention. But each moment is part of a totality. Each moment is a brush stroke in a painting – let's say a painting of a river – which, when we stand back, can be rather beautiful. I have had moments of pain so strong I wanted everything to end. But standing back, they're just shadows accentuating light.

Dam

Let them flow. All those unspoken thoughts. All those suppressed emotions. All those unacknowledged difficulties. All those guilty secrets. All those painful memories. All those hidden corners. All those awkward truths. All those undressed wounds. All those uncomfortable ideas. All those latent longings and denied desires. All that water building behind the dam. Don't wait for that pressure to build. Don't wait to burst wide open. Let them flow. Let them flow. Let them flow.

No man ever steps in the same river twice, for it's not the same river and he's not the same man.

Heraclitus

Elements of hope

Earth, water, fire, air.

Everything connects.

Everything in the universe relates to every other thing in the universe.

'You can't say A is made of B or vice versa,' said the physicist Richard Feynman. 'All mass is interaction.' And maybe what is true for matter is true for psychology and our emotional selves. Pain connects to pleasure through time. A pleasurable present evolves and connects to the pain of grief, when it becomes a memory. But so too, inside deep despair, the knowledge of better times (or even the knowledge of *potential* better times) can help get you through. And sometimes, even within those moments of despair, we can reach pleasure *via the despair.* I have to be careful how I phrase this, as I am not entirely sure I understand it, but there was a kind of pleasure I knew from *inside* depression.

I don't mean to diminish the depression. It was intense, and life-threatening, and I wanted it to end and had no idea when or how it would, but – *but* – despite that – no, *because* of that – when I experienced a moment of beauty or relief it would take on so much power. The night sky would almost sing with beauty. A kiss or a hug would be magnified with meaning. It was almost as though, in those moments, life outside my mind sensed the destructive force within me and was trying to combat it with wonder.

Consider how every human body contains trace elements such as copper and zinc and gold, amid the massive amounts of carbon and oxygen and hydrogen. Similarly, if we could analyse every negative experience we've ever had we would find vast quantities of emotions such as fear and despair, and also trace elements of other things. Joy, hope, love, happiness. And in the darkness even the tiniest fragments of light can shine, capture our attention and maybe even lead us home.

Delete the italics

I am *not popular* enough.
I am *not good* enough.
I am *not strong* enough.
I am *not lovable* enough.
I am *not attractive* enough.
I am *not cool* enough.
I am *not hot* enough.
I am *not clever* enough.
I am *not funny* enough.
I am *not educated* enough.
I am *not Oxford* enough.
I am *not literary* enough.
I am *not rich* enough.
I am *not posh* enough.
I am *not young* enough.
I am *not tough* enough.

I am *not well-travelled* enough.

I am *not talented* enough.

I am *not cultured* enough.

I am *not smooth-skinned* enough.

I am *not thin* enough.

I am *not muscular* enough.

I am *not famous* enough.

I am *not interesting* enough.

I am *not worth* enough.

(I am enough.)

Tips for how to make
a bad day better

Get up. Get washed. Get dressed. Stand up. Move your body. Put your phone in another room. Go for a walk. Stretch. Place your legs against the wall. Get some sunlight, if there is some available. Head, if you can, to somewhere green. A garden, a park, a field, a meadow, a forest. Breathe deeply and slowly and consciously for a little while. Phone someone you love. If there is a nagging thing you are expected to do, but really don't want to do, cancel it now. Do it now. If you can, cook a good meal and concentrate on the process. Cooking is the best kind of active meditation. Avoid artificial blue light, especially after dark. Allow bad thoughts, because that way they pass through quicker. Watch some TV you really like. But before you watch it, work out how long you want to watch for, and stick to it. If it is a clear night, watch the stars, just as Marcus Aurelius did in times of turmoil nearly two thousand years ago. Go to bed before midnight. Don't try too hard to get to sleep. Just allow your mind to absorb the day, and let all those fears and frustrations float through.

The most important kind of wealth

In 1981, American philosophy graduate Steven Callahan found himself adrift in the Atlantic for seventy-six days. He had been sailing a sloop he had designed and built, the *Napoleon Solo*. He was seven days into a voyage from Cornwall to Antigua.

One night, during a storm, the boat was hit by a whale. The boat was quickly flooded and started to sink. Callahan escaped onto an inflatable life raft but also managed to hold his breath and dive down into his boat a few times to get hold of essential supplies. These supplies included a small amount of food, navigation charts, flares, a spear gun and sleeping bag.

He was then set entirely adrift from the boat. He was 800 miles west of the Canary Islands but heading in the opposite direction. He only had enough food and water to last him a few days.

He fished with the spear gun and made water with a solar still, a contraption that evaporates saltwater and distils it and then purifies it. It took him days to get it working properly.

There were many moments of dashed hope. For instance, on the fourteenth day he saw a ship and lit a flare and thought he had been seen. But no such luck. He saw other ships, but again no one saw him, and soon he was south of the shipping lanes, heading into hotter and hotter weather.

The discomfort was immense. The hunger. The thirst. The heat. The saltwater sores on his skin.

Mentally, according to his own accounts, it was also tough. Not just the continual threat of sharks, but his own thoughts.

'I had a lot of time to think, and I regretted every mistake I'd ever made', he told the *Guardian* newspaper in 2012. 'I was divorced, and felt I had failed at human relations generally, at business and now even at sailing. I desperately wanted to get through it so I could make a better job of my life.'

Fifty days in, and things were looking hopeless.

He had spent over a week trying to keep the damaged raft afloat with a pump, and he had no more energy. He broke down. But pulled himself together just enough to find a way to temporarily fix the raft.

Then his contraption to purify his water broke. He knew, logically, he was going to die, as he only had three cans of water left. He felt his mind, as well as his body, shutting down. He had lost a third of his weight. He had nothing else to give. His use of flares and beacons had triggered no rescue attempt.

'I could feel all the people who had ever been lost at sea around me.'

At some point he threw discarded fish guts back into the sea. Which caused seabirds to hover above him.

The seabirds drew the attention of some fishermen from the Guadeloupe archipelago. They found Callahan on his seventy-sixth day on the raft and took him to shore, where he would eventually recover in hospital.

Although the ordeal was terrifying, and nearly cost him his life, Callahan didn't regret having gone through it. And it never put him off sailing.

In his book *Adrift: 76 Days Lost at Sea* he writes of how he no longer regrets his life, and how he has learned to be grateful. 'My plight has given me a strange kind of wealth, the most important kind. I value each moment that is not spent in pain, desperation, hunger, thirst, or loneliness.'

Even more remarkable is his memory of beautiful moments *within* his ordeal. The sight of a clear, starry night sky overwhelmed him with awe. 'A view of heaven from a seat in hell.'

Nothing is stronger than a small hope that doesn't give up.

Nothing is stronger than a small hope that doesn't give up.

Nothing is stronger than a small hope that doesn't give up.

Let everything happen to you: beauty and terror.
Just keep going.
No feeling is final.

Rainer Maria Rilke, *The Book of Hours*

A reminder for the tough times

One day this will be over. And we will be grateful for life in ways we never felt possible before.

The goldsaddle goatfish

The goldsaddle goatfish is a beautiful golden fish – similar in size and behaviour to a red mullet – vulnerable to numerous larger predators, including humans, within the waters around Hawaii. Local divers have recently begun to notice a striking and much larger fish, of an identical yellow-gold colour, swimming in the same sea. When divers swim right next to this big fish it stops being a big fish altogether, breaking up into eight or so standard-sized goldsaddle goatfish. It appears that the fish swim extremely close together, in a perfect fish-shaped pattern, when they feel threatened. Another one of the million examples in nature of how we living creatures shed our vulnerability when we join together and swim as one.

Humans, too, can be saved by each other. Each year's human rights struggles, catastrophes or pandemics are examples of how people pull together in a crisis. How neighbours turn to neighbours. Friends to friends. Allies to allies. We have each other. Togetherness is a rule of nature.

Rain

You don't have to be positive. You don't have to feel guilty about fear or sadness or anger. You don't stop the rain by telling it to stop. Sometimes you just have to let it pour, let it soak you to your skin. It never rains for ever. And know that, however wet you get, you are not the rain. You are not the bad feelings in your head. You are the person *experiencing* the storm. The storm may knock you off your feet. But you will stand again. Hold on.

Truth and courage
and Karl Heinrich Ulrichs

'Be yourself' is perhaps the most common life advice on the planet, yet it is not always easy – or even possible – to follow. Imagine your own gender identity or sexual orientation being met with stigma and criminalisation. Imagine, for instance, being a teenage boy in Germany in the 1830s and realising, without a single doubt, that you were attracted solely to males. Maybe you would try to hide or suppress it, or deny it. It is unlikely you would tell your family. And indeed Karl Heinrich Ulrichs waited until 1862, when he was in his late thirties, before telling his parents he was an *Urning* (a term he himself coined, derived from Plato's *Symposium*) and attracted to men. Once he had taken that step, he took another, bigger one. He began to write about the need for sexual reform. At first he did this anonymously, but soon he did so under his own name. His writings advocating for a scientific understanding of homosexuality continually brought him trouble with the law, and yet he kept writing. He stood in front of the Congress of German Jurists in Munich and demanded the repeal of anti-homosexual laws even as he was shouted down.

Now recognised as a groundbreaking figure in the history of gay rights, Ulrichs had no easy life. His message and campaigning and even his very identity were met with fiery opposition. His books were banned and confiscated by police in Saxony and Berlin and throughout Prussia. Yet his spirit remained unwavering, and not confined to the subject of gay rights either (he was once imprisoned for opposing Prussian rule after the annexation of Hanover). Later his health faltered, so he moved south to Italy, where it improved and where he kept writing and publishing his work at his own expense.

His legacy today is immense. Professor Robert Beachy has referred to him as the first person to publicly 'come out'. There are streets named after him across Germany. The International Lesbian, Gay, Bisexual, Transgender & Intersex Law Association now has an award in his name.

Though the personal cost for Ulrichs was huge, it is clear he had no regrets about being himself. He didn't need to wait for the vindication of the future to realise he had done the right thing in standing up for people marginalised and punished for being themselves. 'Until my dying day', he wrote, nearing the end of his life, 'I will look back with pride that I found the courage to come face to face in battle against the spectre which for time immemorial has been injecting poison into me and into men of my nature. Many have been driven to suicide because all their happiness in life was tainted. Indeed, I am proud that I found the courage to deal the initial blow to the hydra of public contempt.'

It is important to remember that while in our century there remain people ready to stigmatise and criminalise identities and beliefs they don't understand, there are also people like Ulrichs, ready to stand up and be themselves at whatever personal cost. And that is a deep inspiration – indeed a deep comfort – to everyone who has felt stigmatised or marginalised or like their truth is at odds with their time.

Scroll your mind

Social media can be a gallery of lives you aren't living. Of diets you aren't following. Of parties you're not attending. Of holidays you're not on. Of fun you're not having. So, cut yourself a break and scroll your mind instead. Scroll your consciousness for reasons to be grateful to be you. The only fear of missing out that matters is the fear of missing out on yourself.

Current

Even though I have largely recovered from depression, the door is never quite closed, always slightly ajar. I sometimes feel it, light like the ghost of a breeze, very much there. Unseen, but felt. I accept this now but it took time. The binary system of illness and wellness I used to believe in meant you were either one or the other. This was dangerous, because it meant that whenever I began to feel a tiny bit ill again, I would become deeply anxious and depressed that I was back to being properly ill. It would become a self-fulfilling prophecy. I would become ill because I believed I was.

The reality of health, and particularly mental health, is often ambiguous. It is not quite one thing or another. We have a thousand labels for different mild to severe conditions, but reality isn't a simple jar we can stick a label on, to say this is what it is, and it will never change. And nor is mental health something we can clear up once and for all, but rather something we always have to attend to, like a garden that needs nurturing, for as long as we live.

Accepting this is both discomforting *and* comforting. It is discomforting because it means we have to accept that bad feelings and memories can return, and it is comforting because we know that if they do we will be ready for them, and accepting of what they are, transient and changing.

We can move against the current of life, and forever meet resistance, or we can let our thoughts flow, and become the free uncertain river.

Good sad

Do you ever get a kind of gentle sadness that almost feels good? Like a nostalgia for a lost past or a stolen future that is mournful but also reminds you that life is capable of such warm things? And that you were there to witness them?

(I do.)

Jaws and Nietzsche
and death and life

We exist, then we cease to exist. It is okay to feel fear about this. In fact, it might be preferable. As the cultural anthropologist Ernest Becker wrote: 'To live fully is to live with an awareness of the rumble of terror that underlies everything.' Fear is not something to be ashamed of. But fear of death is another fear of the future, another fear of the abstract that takes us away from the present, so the answer to our fear is here, and it is now, and it is real.

When I was in the depths of a breakdown, my fear of life and fear of death were equally matched. I was scared of the pain of living, and I was scared of the annihilation of death. It seems paradoxical but I was never more scared of death than when I was actively suicidal. And the two things seemed intrinsically related.

They were opposites but they were also the same. Fear is compounded by uncertainty and choosing something takes the pain of that uncertainty and turns it into something controllable. It is stupid, really. I wanted to die because I didn't want to die.

It seems to me that the fear of death, like the fear of anything, is made worse when we don't talk about it and make it visible. Fears become stronger when we don't see them. People fear great white sharks, unfairly, because of the film *Jaws*. One of many interesting facts about that seminal summer blockbuster is that we don't see the shark fully until we are one hour and twenty-one minutes into the film, which is way past the halfway point. Now there are boringly practical reasons for that – chiefly that the mechanical shark rarely worked during filming – but that doesn't undermine the point: the shark is scarier for not being seen.

The same, I would say, is true of death. Even more than sex, death is a teeth-grindingly uncomfortable subject for many human beings, certainly those of us living in modern Western cultures. And yet death forms the basis for so many of our deepest concerns.

And it is a part of life. It helps *define* life. It raises the value of our time here, and the value of the people we spend it with. The silence at the end of the song is as important as the song itself.

Or, as Nietzsche put it: 'The end of a melody is not its

goal: but nonetheless, had the melody not reached its end it would not have reached its goal either.'

Underwater

We are where we need to be. We have never lived in the past. There is no past. There is no future. There is just a series of presents. One after the other. And although there are an infinite number of meditations and online tutorials teaching us how to 'inhabit the present', we already do this without trying. We always inhabit the present. 'Forever is composed of nows', as Emily Dickinson told us. So being 'in the now' is something we don't have to work at. When we are imagining our future or mourning the past we aren't in either – we are inhabiting the present, and only the present, because a memory or dream is remembered or dreamed with the tools and texture of the present. It is always today. Yesterday and tomorrow are also todays.

But of course, when we talk about inhabiting the present we mean something else. We are talking about how to actually *enjoy* the present, free from worries. To actually live it the way we imagine some other animals manage to, without fretting about what is to come, or without scrolling through Instagram until our thumb falls off. To *live*. To 'launch yourself on every wave' and 'find your eternity in each moment' in the words of Henry David Thoreau. Though, to be perfectly honest, that sounds a little exhausting and maybe just a tad impractical. There are some moments that are simply going to be a little bit mediocre and un-noticed. The pressure to live so deeply in every moment could also make us feel like we have one more thing to fail at. And the irony for me is that I was closest to finding eternity in every moment when I was suicidally depressed. At that point I was agonisingly aware of being in the moment. And every moment felt like for ever. A day was a lifetime. The waves of time I was being launched into were drowning me. I was underwater and I couldn't breathe.

I would have done anything not to be inside the moment. To be unaware of the moment. To achieve not mindfulness, but total mindlessness. To fast-track into a better future or hitch-hike back to the past.

So, for me, the aim of 'being in the moment' is not enough. I want to be sure that being in the moment won't kill me.

One key barrier to enjoying the present is the fact that a lot of us – me included – are completists. We can't just sit there basking in *being*, because of all those unfinished things. Those unanswered emails, and unpaid bills, and unmet goals. How can we just *be* when there is so much to *do*?

The hardest dream of all to achieve is the dream of not being tormented by our unlived dreams. To cope with and accept unfulfillment as a natural human condition. To be complete in our incompleteness. To be free from the shackles of memory, and ambition, to be free from comparison to other people and other hypothetical selves, and to meet the moment without any other agenda, to exist as freely as time itself.

I hope this email finds you well

I hope this email finds you calm.

I hope this email finds you unflustered about your inbox.

I hope this email finds you in a state of acceptance that this email isn't exactly important in the cosmic scheme of things.

I hope this email finds your work happily unfinished.

I hope this email finds you beneath a beautiful sky with the wind tenderly caressing your hair like an invisible mother.

I hope this email finds you lying on a beach, or maybe beside a lake.

I hope this email finds you with the sunlight on your face.

I hope this email finds you eating some blissfully sweet grapes.

I hope this email finds you well but, you know what, it is okay if it doesn't because we all have bad days.

I hope this email finds you reading a really good poem or something else that requires no direct response from you.
I hope this email finds you far away from this email.

A note on the future

Our anxieties and insecurities, particularly it seems in the West, are shaped by our demand that the future be free from worry. But of course we can't ever have such assurance. The future sits there with pen in hand, refusing to sign that particular contract.

Alan Watts, a British philosopher heavily influenced by Eastern philosophy and spirituality, reminded us that the future is inherently unknown. 'If . . . we cannot live happily without an assured future, we are certainly not adapted to living in a finite world where, despite the best plans, accidents will happen, and where death comes at the end.' So, in other words, if we demand the future be free from suffering in order to be happy, we can't be happy. It is like demanding the sea be entirely still before we sail on it.

Beware because

Your value never needs to be justified. You aren't valuable *because* you work hard or earn a lot or can jump high or have a six-pack or you built a business or you are kind or look good in selfies or present a TV show or can sit at the piano and play 'Für Elise' off by heart. Your value has no because. You are the right quantity. You are a full cup. You are worth yourself, and that is always enough.

Ten things that won't make you happier

1. Wanting to be someone you aren't.
2. Wishing you could undo a past that can't be undone.
3. Taking out your hurt on people who didn't cause your hurt.
4. Trying to distract yourself from pain by doing something that creates more pain.
5. Being unable to forgive yourself.
6. Waiting for people to understand you when they don't even understand themselves.
7. Imagining happiness is the place you reach when you get everything done.
8. Trying to control things in a universe characterised by unpredictability.
9. Avoiding painful memories by resisting a contented present.
10. The belief that you have to be happy.

Check your armour

Check your emotional armour is actually protecting you, and not so heavy you can't move.

Your problem is how you are going to spend this one and precious life you have been issued. Whether you're going to spend it trying to look good and creating the illusion that you have power over circumstances, or whether you are going to taste it, enjoy it and find out the truth about who you are.

Anne Lamott, Berkeley commencement address

A human, being

Your worth is you. Your worth is your presence. Your worth is right there. Your worth isn't something you *earn*. Your worth isn't something you *buy*. Your worth isn't something you gain through *status* or *popularity* or *stomach crunches* or *having a really chic kitchen*. Your worth is your existence. You were born with worth, as all babies are, and that worth doesn't disappear simply because you have grown a little older. You are a human, being.

You are waterproof

It is easier to learn to be soaked and happy than to learn how to stop the rain.

PART THREE

Each of us is born with a box of matches inside us.

Laura Esquivel, *Like Water for Chocolate*

Candle

When things go dark, we can't see what we have. That doesn't mean we don't have those things. Those things remain, right there in front of us. All we need is to light a candle, or ignite some hope, and we can see that what we thought was lost was merely hidden.

A bag of moments

Happy moments are precious. We need to hold on to them. Save them. Write them down. Place them in a bag. Have that metaphorical bag with you, for when it seems happy moments could never exist. Sometimes just to be reminded of happiness makes it more possible.

Your most treasured possession

The present is known. The future is unknown. The present is solid. The future is abstract. Ruining the present by worrying about the future is like burning your most treasured possession simply because you might one day lose other possessions that you don't own yet.

Wolf

Crying releases stress hormones. Swearing increases pain tolerance. Fury can motivate us into action.

Feel what you feel.

Silence and smiles aren't the only way to respond to pain.

Sometimes it is good to howl.

Burn

I once accidentally set fire to my leg.

I was sixteen years old. It was New Year's Eve. I had, quite typically for this period of my existence, drunk a lot of cider.

I was at a sleepover party in a friend's garden. There was a fire outside because it was a cold night, as winter nights tend to be in Nottinghamshire.

Anyway, I was obviously too close to the fire because people were pointing at my leg and shouting wildly and then I looked down and saw my jeans were ablaze.

I quickly patted down my leg and others joined in. The fire was put out but my leg was in agony. I went inside my friend's house and inspected the wound. It covered about a third of my left thigh. Shades of purple. Oozing. Glistening. Disgusting.

'Are you sure you're okay?' people asked.

For reasons I still can't fathom, beyond a deep teenage awkwardness and self-consciousness that was stronger than any pain, I turned down the offer to have an ambulance collect me. But during the night the pain was too intense to sleep, and as I focused on the wound it became increasingly all-encompassing.

So I walked the six miles home, beside a train track. Limping, I was sober now, and the pain was intense – a pulsing kind of pain that was making me delirious.

If we keep going in a straight line we'll get out of here . . .

At one point I had to stop. I sat down and closed my eyes. A freight train thundered past. I thought I would never make it home. But somehow, I did.

As soon as I got home my sister saw the wound. She gasped and nearly fainted and said I needed to go to hospital straight away, and so I went.

My wound was dressed.

'You must never wait in pain,' said the specialist, or words to that effect. It was a message I would think of years later when I was suicidal. 'You must see to it straight away. It doesn't go away by pretending it isn't there.'

Virtue

It is entirely human to be imperfect. It is entirely human to be flawed. It is entirely human to have certain prejudices and have internalised some of the more dubious characteristics of the place and time we live in and the environment we grew up in. No one is above the terrifying and miraculous mess of our species. Humans have the capacity for moments of brilliance and goodness, but also an awful lot of fucking up. If we see problematic people only as 'people other than us', we are never going to have the courage to transform ourselves. And it does take courage. Courage, as Maya Angelou put it, is the most important of the virtues because 'without courage we cannot practice any other virtue with consistency'. Courage is essential for us to look at ourselves without shying away. And, of course, if we make it entirely forbidden to be problematic, we are never going to admit to or address or fix our own flaws with honesty. We need open light to grow. Virtue isn't something we gain simply by pointing to bad things outside ourselves and making ourselves feel good by contrast. True virtue is something we achieve by looking inward, to our own motives and flaws and cravings, and addressing those sticky and difficult and contradictory parts of ourselves.

(Virtue is a journey, not a destination.)

An asymmetric tree is
one hundred per cent a tree

Perfection belongs to another world. Back in ancient Greece, Plato talked about the importance of thinking of ideal forms of things. Ideal love, ideal society, ideal government, ideal shapes. It was important to know how things could be perfect in order to make them better, was the general idea. There might not be such a thing as a perfect square in the whole of nature, but it helps an architect or town planner to know the ideal version of a square so they can take it from the abstract realm and try their best to replicate it. It helps to know what the perfect form of friendship or education or justice might look like, too, so friends and teachers and judges can replicate it.

All great stuff, and I am not about to start a fight with Plato, as he was a wrestler as well as a philosopher apparently, but the problems start when we are told we can reach perfection with the right bank account or app or personal trainer. And then we remain imperfect, as all things are, and we might feel even worse for having believed this perfect Platonic world exists.

Another reason I don't have to fight with Plato is because Aristotle already did. Aristotle, himself a one-time student of Plato's, had a looser, more earth-bound approach to life. He believed that we shouldn't focus on an abstract world of essential forms because this world right here – this one we live on – contains those essential forms. For Plato a tree was always a poor imitation of an ideal tree, whereas for Aristotle a tree always contains its essential tree-ness in its very substance.

The trouble with perfect abstract ideals that we want to reach is that we never get there. They are untouchable rainbows. Far better, I reckon, to find a comfort in the world itself. To try and see trees as essential versions of trees, and ourselves as essential versions of ourselves, and to cultivate the essential spirit of who we are, rather than to reach for something that doesn't and can't exist and watch it forever slip through our fingers.

Work with what you have. Exist in this world. Be the asymmetric square. Be the wonky tree. Be the real you.

You are more than your worst behaviour

If you tell a child they are useless, they'll begin to believe they are useless. If you tell yourself you are useless, the same thing happens. The depressed person who believes that people hate them is more likely to act in ways that fulfil that expectation. And if we believe people must fall into the crudely divided binaries of 'good' and 'bad', we can easily risk judging ourselves forever because of one mistake.

We need kindness. We need a way to see the difference between who people *are* and what they sometimes *do*. And that includes us.

Warm

Don't worry about being cool. Never worry what the cool people think. Life is warmth. You'll be cool when you're dead. Head for the warm people. Head for life.

Dream

Our very existence is a remarkable testimony to human survival. When we think of the likelihood that, after 150,000 generations, we would end up here, alive, right now, as *us*, we are contemplating an improbability so vast it is almost an impossibility. Think of all the terrible and unlikely stories of survival, and of each relative above us in the chain of existence having to stay alive and meet a mate. It is the contemplation of absurd odds. We are all inside a dream that is real. We are the fires conjured from nothing. We exist out of near impossibility. And yet we exist.

Nothing is stronger than a small hope that doesn't give up.

Nothing is stronger than a small hope that doesn't give up.

Nothing is stronger than a small hope that doesn't give up.

Nothing is stronger than a small hope that doesn't give up.

Nothing is stronger than a small hope that doesn't give up.

Nothing is stronger than a—

Clarity

You are here. And that is enough.

The importance of weird thinking

It is good to be weird. It is good to be eccentric. It is good to be separate from the crowd. The philosopher John Stuart Mill thought it was almost a civic duty to be eccentric, to break the tyranny of conformity and custom. But even if we don't feel *outwardly* eccentric, we all have eccentric parts. Thoughts that crop up on the peripheries of our thinking. Random sparks we can set alight. Thoughts that offer the other point of view or the other side of a political argument. Thoughts that don't quite fit in with our other thoughts. Tastes that go against our other tastes. And as we grow older it is good to keep tending to those unconventional parts of ourselves – the thoughts that buck the trend – because these are the parts that will keep us new and capable of surprise. They will stop us becoming a cover version of ourselves. They will help us become new songs.

Outside

Yes, sure, it is comfortable to be on the inside. Sheltered, protected. But there is a comfort to the outside too. Because outside is freedom. Outside you can keep moving until you find a place of your own. Or you can decide that outside *is* your place. And stay there.

Realisation

I used to worry about fitting in until I realised the reason I didn't fit in was because I didn't want to.

The way out of your mind is via the world

By the age of thirty-two, Ludwig van Beethoven's deafness was accelerating fast. He wrote to his brothers to convey his despair that people judged him as 'malevolent, stubborn or misanthropic' when really he was just in a state of inner turmoil due to his advancing condition. He wrote that he felt like a 'hopeless case' because he hadn't been writing much music, which is like Shakespeare calling himself a bit of a slacker for taking a while to write *Hamlet*.

Beethoven recalled times when he was in the countryside and a shepherd was singing or someone was playing a flute and he hadn't been able to hear a thing. Such instances had brought him to despair and he 'would have put an end to my life – only Art it was that withheld me, ah it seemed impossible to leave the world until I had produced all that I felt called upon me to produce . . .'

Only Art it was that withheld me.

And so he stayed alive. Even as his deafness increased – the ultimate torture for the ultimate musician – he continued to create. Indeed, some of his greatest works, such as his brilliantly brooding and atmospheric Piano Sonata No. 14 – commonly known as the 'Moonlight Sonata' – were created when he was entirely deaf.

What a tragic thought that the man who created some of the most well-known music in the world never heard a lot of it. But he had a passion. And the history of the arts is filled with sensitive-minded people who have been consoled and given purpose by the art they create, from Emily Dickinson to Georgia O'Keeffe.

We don't need to write piano sonatas, but what we do need is to be immersed in our passions. It can be anything outside of ourselves. A few years ago, I kid you not, I helped pull myself out of a moderate anxiety patch by getting deeply into the first four seasons of *Game of Thrones*.

Curiosity and passion are the enemies of anxiety. Even when I fall deeply into anxiety, if I get curious enough about something *outside of me* it can help pull me out. Music, art, film, nature, conversation, words.

Find a passion as large as your fear.

The way out of your mind is via the world.

Joy Harjo and the one whole voice

'Everyone comes into the world with a job to do,' wrote Joy Harjo. 'I don't mean working for a company, a corporation – we were all given gifts to share, even the animals, even the plants, minerals, clouds . . . All beings.'

Joy Harjo was born in Tulsa, Oklahoma, and is a member of the Muscogee (Creek) Nation. She is the first Indigenous American to become the United States poet laureate. Her poems are beautiful, and draw on her heritage and the depths of the human subconscious. She is an activist, but her activism isn't confined to one area. She has spoken about the rights of Indigenous Americans, feminism and climate change, and feels these are all interconnected. Indeed, that is a theme of her work. The holistic nature of things. 'To pray you open your whole self / To sky, to earth, to sun, to moon / To one whole voice that is you.'

Harjo embodies this in other ways too. When she performs

she fuses prose and poetry and music as if they are all the same thing. She wrote a piece called 'Ahhhh Saxophone' and with that instrument, she says, 'all that love we humans carry makes a sweet deep sound and we fly a little'.

She has won awards for her music as well as her poetry. The interesting thing is that she was in her forties before she learned to play the saxophone. Well, it's interesting – and comforting – to me because it tells me it is really never too late to begin something valuable.

I abandoned the piano at the age of thirteen. Up until then my parents had been paying for me to attend weekly piano lessons with a piano teacher, Mrs Peters. But then I became the adolescent who didn't want to tell his friends he couldn't see them on Friday evening because he was having piano lessons. Other interests took over my young mind, and learning Beethoven's 'Für Elise' and Mozart's 'Gavotte' seemed suddenly an irrelevant chore.

Many times over the years I have regretted that decision, wondering what it would have been like if I had kept going. And yet, for all that wondering, I never actively did anything about it until this year, at the age of forty-five, when I began to re-learn the piano with my kids during lockdown. Of course, it is humiliating trying to learn *anything* side-by-side with an eleven- and twelve-year-old. It is like trying to learn to swim beside a sailfish. But it was great to make progress, to actually play, and to realise that there is no cut-off age for development.

Joy Harjo is not the only musical late starter, of course. Leonard Cohen famously didn't begin his musical career until deep in his thirties. Though gifted musically from a young age, Verdi wrote most of his best stuff after the age of fifty, including his opera of *Otello* which he finished aged seventy-three.

I will never be as musically competent as Verdi, or Joy Harjo, or even, as it turns out, a fast-learning twelve-year-old, but I have access to the ability to play music, and enjoy playing music, and that is enough. The joy of music is in the music. The playing of it. The listening to it. And it is a joy with a wide-open door, welcoming all.

That's all we can do, right? Keep as many doors open as possible. Keep embracing the whole of ourselves. Keep failing. As Harjo herself says, 'there is no poetry where there are no mistakes'.

Protection

Once upon a time I felt pressure not to let people down. I stayed doing work I hated. Went to parties I didn't really want to be at. Saw people I found agonisingly hard to converse with. Faked every smile.

And then my mind exploded.

After which I realised it is better to let people down than to blow yourself up.

Quantum freedom

According to quantum physics, the laws of the universe are probabilistic. This means that even among the smallest particles, nothing is entirely predictable. There is always uncertainty and things that can't be entirely predicted and measured. Determinism fails in the face of quantum reality. The German physicist Werner Heisenberg, who came up with the uncertainty principle – or rather, the Uncertainty Principle – discovered that even if every single initial condition is known, it is still impossible to predict with any fixed certainty the behaviour of waves and particles. Likewise, chaos theory explains how even things on a bigger scale, like weather, are not entirely predictable and can't ever be. (How many times have we been surprised by a day of sunshine when we were told to expect showers?) Similarly, neuroscientists have shown us that the very structure of our brain, and the nerve cells within it, also acts with elements of randomness.

In other words, a key defining feature of the universe, of nature, of our environment, of *us*, is uncertainty. There is always a space for chance. As something begins to change or move, it changes with a degree of the unknown, whether it is light through a slit in a barrier or a hurricane or a brain cell. The universe is, essentially, an ever-evolving possibility. While fear might want us to imagine the worst is certain, the future – like everything else – remains uncertain, unpredictable, open, free. And even the very smallest event in the maze that is our lives can result in the most unexpected outcome.

Other people are other people

Let's state the obvious, because the obvious is easy to take for granted and forget. You are not other people. You are you. You have no control over other people. You have no absolute control over what they think of the world or of politics or of you. You have no control over what harm they may have done. Even if the harm they have done is to you. Yes, of course we can often learn from each other, and sometimes people learn from you. And that's great, even if it is rarer than we like to admit. As Ayishat Akanbi put it, 'If you've decided your healing is dependent on other people acknowledging their faults you'll still be waiting in your grave.' You don't punish anyone other than yourself by keeping hate inside you. Other people are other people. You are you.

Wrong direction

Your self-worth is not found inside the minds of other people.

Applied energy

History can be a comfort. It helps us understand our place in time, and to appreciate what humans have done and lived through in the past for us to end up here.

Discovering the human stories of the past, in particular, can give us a kind of strength. Knowing what human beings achieved, what they survived, and that some of them managed to make the world better for us to live in today.

Have you heard of Nellie Bly?

She was one of the most inspiring journalists ever to have lived.

Nellie Bly was in fact a pen name. When she was born in Pittsburgh in 1864 she was christened Elizabeth Jane Cochran. After her father died when she was fifteen, she and her mother and fourteen siblings were left with little money and so Bly went out to try and earn some.

At a time when women were a rare and actively discouraged sight in journalism, Bly managed to get a job for her local newspaper, earning five dollars a week. However, she was told she was only to write about domestic things like childcare and housework. Despite that, the popularity of her column allowed her to start writing in a more investigative way, and she moved onto meatier issues such as the impact of divorce laws on women.

In 1887 she moved to New York and managed to meet the famous newspaper publisher Joseph Pulitzer. She wanted to work for his publication, *New York World*, but in a test of her commitment he said that her first piece would be an investigation into conditions at Blackwell's Island Asylum, a notorious 'lunatic' asylum for women. The catch was that Bly would need to go undercover. In other words, she would need to pretend to be insane and get committed there.

This was no easy task. She checked into a boarding house called Temporary Homes for Females and stayed up all night to give herself a drained and dishevelled appearance. Then she put on a wild-eyed act of insanity, and – following psychiatric evaluation – was sent to the asylum.

There, she experienced and witnessed hellish conditions. Bullying staff. Mentally ill women tied up together with ropes. Rat-infested wards. Rotten food. Dirty drinking water. Shared bath water. Hard benches. Cruel punishments. One of the things she quickly noted was that many of the women didn't seem insane at all yet were treated horrifically. Bly believed that a few hours of being there would test the mind of any sane person.

From the moment she arrived Bly dropped her act of insanity and acted as she normally would. Yet she noticed that every normal thing she did – like ask the staff if they had taken her pencil – was treated as further proof of insanity: 'The more sanely I talked and acted the crazier I was thought to be.' She also witnessed the most severely ill patients being actively provoked.

It was ten days before the *New York World* told the asylum the truth, and that their reporter should be released. It was a harrowing assignment. Yet by witnessing and writing about her experience, Bly helped shift the American public's view of asylums and mental illness.

As a direct result of her two-part article 'Ten Days in a Mad House', the state department in charge of the asylum had its budget raised by a million dollars. Even more impressive, her list of recommendations was taken on board by the Department of Public Charities and Correction, and this resulted in the closure of the asylum a few years later.

Nellie Bly became famous. And helped usher in a new age of intense, undercover journalism.

She went on to report all kinds of dramatic stories, a far cry from the kind of domestic fare she had initially been encouraged to write about in Pittsburgh. She covered everything from government corruption to baby-buying scandals.

In 1889 she became even more famous as the person who broke the fictional record set by Phileas Fogg in the Jules Verne novel *Around the World in Eighty Days*, when she embarked on a 24,900-mile trip around the globe and completed it in a whisker over seventy-two days. While on the trip she met Jules Verne in Paris, visited a leper colony in China and journeyed along the Suez Canal. She travelled on boats and trains and even the occasional donkey.

The remarkable thing is that even as other people were sent out to beat her, she refused to treat it as a race. And her reporting shows how much she appreciated every moment of beauty in her journey. 'I always liked fog', she wrote, 'it lends such a soft, beautifying light to things that otherwise in the broad glare of day would be rude and commonplace.'

Years later, during the First World War, she became the first female reporter to visit the conflict zone between Serbia and Austria, and was even arrested – but quickly freed – when she was mistaken for a British spy.

Nowadays her legacy lives on, and she has had all kinds of things named after her: press awards, boats, an ice cream parlour, even an amusement park.

A testimony to what a human can do, armed with little more than a sharp pencil and a sharper mind.

As Bly herself put it, 'Energy rightly applied and directed will accomplish anything.'

She had resisted every role society had wanted her to fit into and became who she wanted to be.

Mess

The hardest thing to be is yourself. We are so overloaded that we can't always see the truth of who we are. We distract ourselves to distraction. Sometimes we clutter our lives deliberately to take our minds off the clutter inside our heads. When we take the external clutter away, we have to face the clutter inside ourselves. All the mess. And the more we focus on it, the more we see the order in it. There is a reason why everything is where it is. We might want to order the mess a different way, or we might feel the mess is perfectly fine. But we are imperfect because we are alive.

We are messy because the universe began with an explosion and the debris has drifted ever since. We are all messy mammals on a messy planet in a messy cosmos. To deny mess is to deny who we are. To see it, to allow it, to forgive it, is to reach a state of what Buddhist and psychologist

166

Tara Brach calls 'radical acceptance', where we can appreciate our so-called flaws or imperfections as a natural part of existence. And then we can exist with openness and honesty, rather than shrink ourselves by trying to shut ourselves away like the contents of a cluttered cupboard. We can, in short, live.

Aim to be you

If you aim to be something you are not, you will always fail. Aim to be you. Aim to look and act and think like you. Embrace that you-ness. Endorse it. Cherish it. Love it. And don't give a fuck if people mock you for it.

Cup

You have no control over who people think you are. So don't worry. If they want to hate a fictional version of you that lives in their minds, let them. Don't drain yourself trying to be understood by people who insist on not understanding you. Keep your cup full. Go to the kindness.

Pomegranate

Much of gossip is envy in disguise. Much of self-doubt is conformity in disguise. 'No one can make you feel inferior without your consent', said Eleanor Roosevelt. Breathe into you. Step out of the shade. Be you in the wide open. The only success that matters is the success of being who you are. Fitting in is fine. But never try and fit in if this fitting-in means becoming something you are not. Become you. Become the person no one else is. If people don't like you, let them not like you. Not every fruit has to be an apple. It is too exhausting to spend this existence as someone else. If you are a pomegranate, be a pomegranate. Sure, there are probably more people who don't like pomegranates than people who don't like apples, but for those of us who like pomegranates they are what we like best.

Let it be

Get out of your own way. Being yourself isn't something you have to do. You were born yourself, and you didn't even have to try. In fact, trying is the whole problem. You can't *try* to *be*. You can only let yourself be.

PART FOUR

Sometimes as an antidote
To fear of death,
I eat the stars.

Rebecca Elson, 'Antidotes to Fear of Death',
A Responsibility to Awe

The sky

Imagine if you had never seen the night sky.

Imagine if the night sky only existed once in every lifetime. Imagine if you could only once look up and see those stars. It would probably be one of the highlights of your existence. It would possibly be known as The Night of Starry Miracles or The Amazing Moment of Witnessing the Shining Universe, or something a bit catchier. We would all step away from our sofas and another evening spent in front of our streaming service of choice and head outside and look upwards, open-mouthed in wonder at the thousands of pinpoints of light sent through time and space. We would be there gazing at the moon and trying to distinguish stars from planets. Wondering which one was Venus.

The point is, it would be nearly impossible to take the sight of such a one-off sky for granted.

And yet we obviously take the night sky for granted. And

of course it would be entirely impractical to suggest that – even on cloudless nights with low light pollution – we should be out there gazing up in sentimental wonder at constellations. But it is always good to know how wonderful so much of life would instantly seem if it was made rare. We are so blessed with an abundance of wonder on this planet, and in this universe, that we are numb to it. And it is often only in times of intense crisis that such things become apparent. That we can each see ourselves, in philosopher Alan Watts' phrase, as 'an aperture through which the universe is looking at and exploring itself'.

Watch the stars

I can remember one night in the middle of a depression feeling suicidal and looking up at a cloudless sky of infinite stars. I felt a mental pain so deep it was physical. But seeing the sky, our small glimpse of the universe, flooded me with hope that I would one day be able to appreciate such a sight again. Beauty is any moment that makes us gasp with the hope and wonder of life, and the world is full of such moments. They shine in the dark. And they are ours for the taking. 'Dwell on the beauty of life', wrote Marcus Aurelius in his *Meditations* two millennia ago, 'watch the stars, and see yourself running with them'.

The universe is change

When he wrote *Meditations*, Marcus Aurelius was the most powerful man in the world. He had, quite literally, a whole empire at his disposal. Cities, armies, palaces. All were his. He spent over a decade, from the year 161 to 180, as Roman emperor during the 'Golden Age'. And yet he resisted seeking any contentment in his status and power, in favour of simplicity, consultation and a cosmic perspective. He believed watching the stars was important and talks about Pythagoras – the early Greek philosopher and founder of Pythagoreanism – as his influence here.

The Pythagoreans saw gazing up at the sky not just as a pleasant thing to do, but an insight into a divine order. Because stars are all separate, but all together in an order. For the Stoics, looking at them was looking at unveiled glimpses of divinity – and also fragments of Nature.

It is not just the sky or the stars, then, that are important, but what we think when we look at them. Our connection to the shifting world around and above us.

'The universe is change', wrote Marcus Aurelius. 'Our life is what our thoughts make it.'

Even a man in charge of an empire could look at the stars and feel happily small in the grand universal order of things.

The sky doesn't start above us. There is no starting point for sky. We live in the sky.

The Stoic slave

My all-time favourite philosopher is Epictetus. Like Marcus Aurelius, he was a Stoic who lived in Ancient Rome. Unlike Marcus Aurelius, he wasn't an emperor. In fact, he was about as far away from an emperor as you can get.

He had a tough life. Born into slavery almost two thousand years ago, his name literally meant 'acquired'. He spent all his youth as a slave, though he was allowed to study Stoic philosophy. He was also physically disabled – possibly due to his leg being broken by his master. He spent most of his life in physical pain.

Epictetus eventually became a free man, for reasons that aren't clear, and began to teach philosophy, but even then he lived very simply, with few possessions, and lived alone for much of his life. Records show that in his old age he adopted a child of a friend and raised that child with a woman whom Epictetus may or may not have married.

Epictetus was a very modern philosopher in some ways. His worldview is probably best summed up by his statement 'It's not what happens to you, but how you react that matters.' It is a philosophy that has been credited with helping people in tough circumstances, from prisoners of war to people experiencing depression. The psychologist Albert Ellis, one of the originators of cognitive behavioural therapy, cites this Epictetus quote as influencing his entire therapeutic approach: 'Man is disturbed not by things, but by the views he takes of them.'

Epictetus reminds us that when we tie our happiness to external things, we are essentially giving up the idea of self-control and placing our well-being on forces outside of ourselves. Whatever it is – earnings, relationships, wanting a family, a Lamborghini, winning the lottery, going viral on social media – 'Just keep in mind: the more we value things outside our control, the less control we have.' And of course, even when we get the things we think we want, the impact is often beyond our prediction – see, for instance, the studies into how winning the lottery often has a negative impact on the winner's happiness.

The comfort of Epictetus is the deepest comfort there is. It isn't the reassurance of believing great things will happen to us, it is that of knowing that even in pain or sadness or confinement, the mind has power to choose its response to the events in our lives. Even the very biggest things. Pain, loss, grief, death. 'I cannot escape death', he said, 'but at least I can escape the fear of it.' Epictetus, in short, gives us control in an uncontrollable world. The control of accepting a lack of control. The control of response.

Caterpillar

In the dark cocoon, a caterpillar falls apart. It disintegrates in its own enzymes. It becomes liquid. Mush. Caterpillar soup. And then, slowly, it is reborn a butterfly. Cocoons aren't a cosy quiet resting place. Cocoons must feel a pretty horrendous place for a caterpillar. Yet, the caterpillar's fate has proven a great metaphor for our own misfortunes and struggles. The greatest changes stem from the darkest experiences. We fall apart to become new. We go through the dark to fly in the sun.

Experience

We are not what we experience.

If we stand in a hurricane, it doesn't matter how violent or terrifying the hurricane is, we always know that the hurricane is not us. The weather outside and inside us is never permanent. People talk about dark clouds over them. But we are never the clouds; we are the sky. We just contain them. The clouds are just the present view. The sky stays the sky.

A bit about breathing

I want to tell you that breathing is deeply important.

I know, I know.

This makes me 'that person'. The person who tells you to think about your breathing as if all the problems in the world are caused by an inability to exhale for a count of five. It makes me a millimetre away from being someone who will tell you that handling your trauma is something that can be done via a long bath and a couple of lavender-scented candles. And yet I have realised over the years that there is no quicker indicator of where my stress levels are at than checking where my breathing is at.

Breath is a kind of in-built mood barometer.

When I used to have full-blown panic attacks, breathing was hard. It was something that happened rapid-fire, right at the top of my lungs, as if I didn't even have time for air. When I am stressed I can lie in bed and place my hand on my stomach and take a deep breath and then, towards the end, my stomach will quiver like a frightened animal, and I will know. I will know that now is the time to step back and allow myself to relax. It sounds like a paradox, but making the effort to relax can sometimes work. And the easiest and quickest way for me is through slow breathing. When I make myself breathe slowly it is as if the annoying voices in my mind – the ones that play on rotation like annoying YouTube rants – are suddenly quiet. It becomes almost instantly okay that I didn't get back to that email, or that I messed up a Zoom meeting. I can feel myself stilling.

Breathing consciously seems to be a way to hack into your self-esteem. A way to say *Give yourself a break.* A way to just accept you as you and life as life. And all you need is a pair of lungs.

You can do it lying down or sitting or standing. If I am lying down, I place my arms by my side, palms facing the sky or ceiling, and have my feet a little way apart. If I am sitting, I rest my arms on the chair and have my feet hip-width apart. Then I breathe gently but deeply into my stomach. And yes, I count to five, silently, because the trance-like focus of the counting itself seems to have an added relaxing effect. And ideally I do this for over a minute. If you have five minutes, seriously, try and do it for five minutes. Hell, even longer. It can feel boring at first – because a busy brain wants nothing less and needs nothing more than to slow down – but it is worth it.

You are here. You exist. You are in this moment.

To breathe is to live, I suppose, and to be aware of breathing is to be aware of living, to be aware of the very simplest truth of yourself, and transcend the world of doing and – for a few sweet, comforting moments – inhabit the world of being.

What your breath tells you

You are enough.

You need no more than you. You are more than how you are seen. You are who you are in the dark. You are who you are in the silence. You do not need to buy or train or earn your acceptance.

You are enough.

You are a cosmic miracle. You are the earth witnessing itself. You inhale the air and accept yourself as you accept that air, as a part of the natural order of things. You are the mind that exists in the act of changing. You are possibility in motion. You belong here. You are where you need to be.

You are enough.

Nothing is stronger than a small hope that doesn't give up.

Nothing is stronger than a small hope that doesn't give up.

Nothing is stronger than a small hope that doesn't give up.

Nothing is stronger than a small hope that doesn't give up.

Nothing is stronger than a small hope that doesn't give up.

Nothing is stronger than a small hope that doesn't give up.

Nothing is stronger than a small hope that doesn't give up.

Nothing is stronger than a small hope that doesn't give up.

Nothing is stronger than a small hope that doesn't give up.

Nothing is stronger than a small hope that doesn't give up.

Nothing is stronger than a small hope that doesn't give up.

Nothing is stronger than a small hope that doesn't give up.

Nothing is stronger than a small hope that doesn't give up.

Nothing is stronger than a small hope that doesn't give up.

Nothing is stronger than a small hope that doesn't give up.

Live in the raw

The true challenge we face is to look at ourselves and the world honestly. To see what wounds there are, so we can help heal them. Not to flinch. Not to spend our life wrapped in denial and trying to avoid pain. Not to avoid the feelings. As Buddhist writer Pema Chödrön put it, 'the most fundamental harm we can do to ourselves, is to remain ignorant by not having the courage and the respect to look at ourselves honestly and gently'. Healing means to live in the raw.

Honest seeing

Ignorance shrinks us. The true challenge we face is to look at ourselves and the world honestly. One of the challenges Marcus Aurelius set himself was 'to look things in the face and know them for what they are'.

Wait

You are okay. You may feel like you are in a nightmare. Your mind might be beating you up. You may think you aren't going to make it. But remember a time you felt bad before. And think of something good that happened since, in the interim. That specific goodness may or may not happen again, but *some* goodness will. Just wait.

The cure for loneliness

Loneliness isn't an absence of company. Loneliness is felt when we are lost. But we can be lost right in the middle of a crowd. There is nothing lonelier than being with people who aren't on your wavelength. The cure for loneliness isn't more people. The cure for loneliness is understanding who we are.

Patterns

It is easy to get stuck in a pattern of behaviour. Think of the people you know. Do they do some of the same things over and over? Do they like the same kind of food and drink? Watch the same kind of TV? Read the same genre of books? Do they get up and go to bed at roughly the same time? Do they say the same kinds of things? Have the same kinds of thoughts? Do you? Do I? Yes. To be human – to be alive – is to fall into patterns of behaviour. Some of these patterns are good. We are drawn to the comfort of routine, and we settle in, but there can also be a discomfort in going through the same motions. Just as slumping for hours in the same position can be bad for our backs, it is also true that taking the familiar and repetitive path of least resistance can cause our lives to become a bit stuck in place. We become outdated algorithms needing a new and bigger sequence.

The act of changing our routine is good for us. Even something as simple as rearranging apps on a phone helps us to resist the automatic default of muscle memory.

As Tara Brach put it: 'Perhaps the biggest tragedy in our lives is that freedom is possible, yet we can pass our years trapped in the same old patterns . . . We may want to love other people without holding back, to feel authentic, to breathe in the beauty around us, to dance and sing. Yet each day we listen to inner voices that keep our life small.'

The discomfort zone

A kind of timidity can set in with familiarity. A fear of change. We can end up stuck in jobs we don't like, in unhealthy relationships, with similar unhelpful attitudes. We call this the 'comfort zone' but often it is the opposite. A discomfort zone, a stagnation zone, an unfulfilled zone. It is surprisingly easy to walk through and out, once we decide to. And what we see beyond the discomfort zone is in fact a deeper comfort. The comfort of being the best possible version of us. Beyond the pattern or code of established behaviour. Less coded, more human.

Stuff

You don't always have to do stuff. Or achieve stuff. You don't have to spend your free time productively. You don't have to be doing Tai Chi and DIY and bread-making. Sometimes you can just *be* and *feel things* and get through and eat crisps and survive, and that is more than enough.

Ferris Bueller and the meaning of life

Ferris Bueller's Day Off (1986) is the best teen movie of all time but for years I had a problem with it, even though I enjoyed it immensely. John Hughes's tale of a popular teenager skipping school by faking illness, then having a sensational day out in Chicago with his best friend and girlfriend, annoyed me because I thought Ferris was selfish and this seemed like a movie where liking the central character was essential for its enjoyment. My issue was that he uses his best friend, Cameron, by making him take his dad's vintage Ferrari on their adventure, even though Cameron will get in major trouble for this.

Re-watching the movie, though, I realised I'd got it all wrong. Really, this isn't a movie about the eponymous Ferris. This is a movie about Cameron. Cameron is the emotional centre of the film. He is the one who makes the most significant transition – from a depressed, possibly suicidal, outwardly privileged teenager who frets about the perceived meaninglessness of a future containing college and adulthood, to someone with self-esteem, who is able to live in the present, and to stand up to his strict father and his oppressive rules.

When Ferris starts the movie with his famous monologue he talks straight to the camera, but the core message is one he spends the rest of the film teaching Cameron: 'Life moves pretty fast. If you don't stop and look around once in a while, you could miss it.' Ferris is basically a 1980s version of Marcus Aurelius saying, 'Dwell on the beauty of life.' He is a mix of Eastern and Western philosophy. Buddhist mindfulness fused with American individualism – though he wouldn't want to be part of any -ism. 'A person shouldn't believe in an -ism,' says Ferris. 'He should believe in himself.' But Ferris isn't just out for himself. He is out for his friend too. He is out for us. As with all the most comforting films, the film gives us permission to feel. It helps us live.

Films that comfort

Jaws. Because it shows that we need to acknowledge our fears before we beat them.

Meet Me in St Louis. Because of the songs. Because of the colours. Because of Judy Garland singing 'Have Yourself a Merry Little Christmas'. Because it invites us into the beautiful and bittersweet comfort of another time, another place, another family, another reality. And because I watched it on a day I felt terrible and it gave me a better place to exist.

The Great Escape. Because it shows that you can cope with any situation so long as you are building a tunnel out of it.

Butch Cassidy and the Sundance Kid. Because it exudes a golden fireside glow and makes us remember that we can live for ever inside a freeze-frame if it is a good enough moment (see also the end of *The 400 Blows* and *The Breakfast Club*).

E.T. Because you become a child again when you watch it.

It's a Wonderful Life. Because it makes you realise your existence has unseen value.

The Peanut Butter Falcon. Because it shows the redemptive power of friendship.

The Count of Monte Cristo (2002 version). Because this swashbuckling adventure is the definition of escapism.

Pretty in Pink. Because it has the greatest pop soundtrack in the history of cinema.

Ray. Because well-crafted biopics are always inspiring, especially when the subject is Ray Charles.

My Neighbour Totoro. Because Hayao Miyazaki's masterpiece is a film about the power of wonder and magic to comfort us through traumatic times.

Harvey. Because it is James Stewart talking to an invisible rabbit.

Breaking Away. Because it is a highly underrated film about cycling that I watched when I was feeling low and found solace in its gentle comedy and drama.

Any *Mission Impossible* movie. Because there is something comforting about watching Tom Cruise risk his life to defy the laws of Newtonian physics.

The Sound of Music. Because it shows how love and music and joy can't be suppressed by the darkest forces in history.

Bringing Up Baby. Because of Katharine Hepburn and Cary Grant and because, despite being released in 1938, it remains one of the funniest films ever made.

Toy Story 2. Because it is the greatest and most emotional and consoling Pixar movie, for Jessie's story alone.

Stand By Me. Because despite being a film about a search for a dead body, it is a celebration of youth and friendship and life.

Mary Poppins. Because it is *Mary Poppins*.

Negative capability

The poet John Keats coined the phrase 'negative capability': meaning when someone 'is capable of being in uncertainties, mysteries, doubts, without any irritable reaching after fact and reason'. It's about embracing a kind of vulnerability.

For Keats, Shakespeare was the person who embodied this concept perfectly, as he created work that was full of a beauty that was incomplete and ambiguous and allowed for many possible meanings.

Keats never heard Miles Davis play, but maybe he'd have recognised negative capability in his music. 'Don't play what's there,' the musician famously said. 'Play what's not there.'

Negative capability is about the space *beyond* what we know, which we should be prepared to reach if we want to find beauty.

'With a great poet', wrote Keats, the most Zen of the

Romantics, 'the sense of Beauty overcomes every other consideration, or rather obliterates all consideration.'

Keats's use of negative capability was primarily about art, but it was later adopted by the psychoanalyst Wilfred Bion, who gave it a more psychological and existential slant. For Bion, negative capability was about being able to think intuitively, outside of memory and desire. 'Discard your memory', he implored. 'Discard the future tense of your desire; forget . . . both what you knew and what you want, to leave space for a new idea.'

A new idea.

I love that. It's like the Zen Buddhist concept of *satori*, of enlightenment through submission, something reached through a quest into the uncertainties of our own nature. That is where freedom lives. In the possibility of a new way of thinking. And it is easier to get there if we keep open and ambiguous and alert to the fluidity of the moment.

Maybe we only exist because of some cosmic negative capability that conjured the universe into being out of the void.

It is okay not to know everything. It might be better and wiser not to know everything, or at least to avoid thinking we know everything, because then we are freer from habitual thinking. But sure, it takes a vulnerability to enter a place of total openness, and maybe a new and deeper under-standing of comfort.

I always remember once, years ago, doing a workout

video where the instructor bellowed an order, midway through a static squat, to 'get comfortable with being uncomfortable'. Now, it may be a bit of a reach to equate advice offered in a workout to negative capability and Zen Buddhism, but I feel we reach a higher kind of comfort, a closer union with who we actually are, when we are willing to move out of safe and known patterns towards – to be Keatsian about it – the unknowing beauty of life.

As Wilfred Bion put it, 'Beauty makes a very difficult situation tolerable.'

We don't have to work everything out. We can just witness the beauty.

Why break when you can bend?

You don't have to cope with everything. You don't have to handle everything. You don't have to keep a lid on everything to get through a day.

You can't turn tides. You can't defy gravity. You can't go against the grain without getting splinters.

But you can drop the disguise. You can feel what you feel. You can stretch out inside yourself.

You can cry. You can feel. You can show what you are.

You can, in fact, be you.

We have more in common than we think

It is easy to hate everyone these days. It's easy to go on the internet or switch on the news and feel despair. It's easy to find reasons to be angry. We have social media apps whose very business model depends on our ongoing capacity for fury and frustration.

It's easy to be surrounded so entirely by a single view that almost anyone without that view becomes alien.

But.

We can look at the world through more than one lens. If we look at people through the lens of emotion, at the feelings that drive opinions, rather than the opinions themselves, it's easy to see the things we share. The hopes, the fears, the loves, the insecurities, the longings, the doubts, the dreams.

Other people can be wrong, and we can be wrong, and that is another thing we have in common.

The capacity for fucking up. And for forgiving.

Forgiveness

Forgiving other people is great practice for forgiving your-self when the time comes.

A note on introversion

Introversion is not something you fix via extroversion. You fix it by seeing it as something not to be fixed. Let introversion exist. Allow journeys inward as well as outward.

Resting is doing

You don't need to be *busy*. You don't need to justify your existence in terms of productivity. Rest is an essential part of survival. An essential part of us. An essential part of being the animals we are. When a dog lies in the sun I imagine it does it without guilt, because as far as I can tell dogs seem more in tune with their own needs. As I grow older, I think that resting might actually be the main point of life. To sit down passively, inside or outside, and merely absorb things – the tick of a clock, a cloud passing by, the distant hum of traffic, a bird singing – can feel like an end in itself. It can actually feel and *be* more meaningful than a lot of the stuff we are conditioned to see as *productive*. Just as we need pauses between notes for music to sound good, and just as we need punctuation in a sentence for it to be coherent, we should see rest and reflection and passivity – and even sitting on the sofa – as an intrinsic and essential part of life that is needed for the whole to make sense.

Mystery

Think of the works of art that stand the test of time, from the *Mona Lisa* to *Middlemarch*. There is always something unsolvable about them. Something critics can debate passionately centuries later with no final certainty. Maybe the art of living is like that too. Maybe the purpose *is* the mystery, not beyond it. Maybe we aren't meant to know everything about our lives. And maybe that's perfectly okay.

The comfort of uncertainty

Uncertainty feeds our anxiety. Uncertainty and anxiety are intrinsically linked. The more anxious we are, the harder we will find tolerating uncertainty. We might write lists, avoid delegating. We might seek constant reassurance. We might double check that we locked the door, or repeatedly want to call someone to check they are okay. We might find ourselves clasping control and unwilling to trust others. We might want to retreat from an anxious world and stay indoors and procrastinate. We might want to escape it altogether by losing ourselves in a world of distraction. We might fill every second of our day with busy activities, with work, with pleasure, with our other addictions.

Of course, none of these things address the root problem. Uncertainty still remains. The only way, ultimately, to deal with uncertainty is to accept uncertainty. Because we can't escape it. However we choose to timetable our days and our calendars, uncertainty still remains. This is a stubbornly uncertain world, and we have to deal with that.

And one way to deal with it is to see the value in uncertainty. Far from being a curse, uncertainty can be a source of hope. Okay, so yes, it means that the things we are looking forward to might not be as good as we want them to be, but it also means that the things we dread might not be as terrible as we imagine.

For instance, how many times have you heard people talk about blessings in disguise? How many times have we heard about someone who has been afflicted with a terrible misfortune – an illness, a redundancy, a bankruptcy, whatever – then ends up feeling thankful for it, or at least for some aspect of it?

The moments of deepest pain in my life were also the moments I learned the most about myself. Just as some of the things we look forward to aren't as good as we planned – like a disastrous holiday, or a nightmare job that sounded good on paper, a marriage that turned sour – so it is true that many of the hard things in life arrive with lessons or silver linings or a welcome new perspective or reasons to be grateful.

So, while we see uncertainty as innately unwanted, because it means bad things might happen, uncertainty is also our protection against bad things. Because at some point, in any life, something bad will happen, and it is the inherent uncertainty of what that bad thing will ultimately mean to you, what it will lead to, and what it will reveal, that enables us to have a more enduring and resilient kind of hope. A hope that doesn't wish for bad things not to happen – because they sometimes do – but rather one that enables us to see that bad things are never the whole story. They are as filled with uncertain outcomes as everything else.

In short, we never know. The only certainty is uncertainty. And so, if we are to reach any kind of constant comfort, we need to find comfort in uncertainty. And it is there. Because while things are uncertain, they are never closed. We can exist in hope, in the infinite, in the unanswered and open question of life itself.

Portal

Each of us has the power to enter a new world. All we have to do is change our mind.

Nothing is closed

One of the reasons we like stories is because we like structure. We like a beginning, a middle and an end. We especially like a good ending. Think of all the times our opinion of a book or a movie has hinged on the ending. If a movie has a terrible ending it often ruins the whole thing for us.

The film director Jean-Luc Godard said a story should have a beginning, middle and end, but not necessarily in that order. And I used to love that quote, and agree with it, until I went through a breakdown and craved the comfort of classic narratives. Of beginnings and middles and ends *in that order.* And I liked endings that wrapped things up nicely, with a big bow.

I craved *resolution.* But of course, life doesn't really have a resolution. Even death isn't a resolution. Even if we don't believe in an afterlife, we have to acknowledge that the world after us goes on in unknowable ways, and also the ways people will or will not remember us are unknowable too.

There are only open endings in life. And this isn't a curse. This is a good thing. As the Buddhist thinker Pema Chödrön puts it, 'we suffer from resolution'. I find that idea so liberating. To admit that closure is unreachable in a universe where everything is open.

The bearable rightness of being

Being > doing

Reconnection

My anxiety feels very much a symptom of modern life. At its deepest, years ago, I began to notice that it was always at its most acute when I was doing something that would have been entirely alien to our cave-people ancestors. Walking in a crowded shopping centre. Listening to loud techno music. Wandering under the artificial light of a supermarket. Sitting for too long in front of a TV or computer screen. Eating a bag of tortilla chips at one in the morning. Stressful emails. City centres. Packed trains. Online squabbles. Modern mental overload.

It is no coincidence that the things that comfort me when I am super-frazzled, the things that calm and soothe me, tend to be things that reconnect me to my natural self. So, for instance, going to bed shortly after it gets dark rather than staying up till one a.m. to watch eleven episodes of a TV show one after the other. Or walking in nature with our dog. Or cooking real food with real ingredients. Or being with loved ones. Or switching from the sofa to physical activity. Or planting some herbs. Or swimming in the sea. Or staring at the sky. Or running in the fresh air rather than on the treadmill.

Of course, I love the pleasurable distractions of modern life. I like that our world is one with podcasts and movies and video calls. But when I am in that state of deep fragility, where I am stripped of my shell, I find the shortest path back seems to be the timeless one. The natural one. The one to do with reconnection to our natural world and our natural selves.

A note on joy

On Madonna's first trip to New York she is said to have told her taxi driver, 'Take me to the centre of everything.' For many years before my breakdown that was my approach too. I had trouble with just *being*. I always wanted to be somewhere else, closer to the centre of the excitement. So I escaped into alcohol. Drugs. Raves. I needed the loudest noise, the spiciest food, the most violent movies, the most extreme *everything*. For me this meant three summers in Ibiza working for the largest club night in Europe, being at the centre of noise and people and stimulation. The fact that the night was called 'Manumission', which meant 'freedom from slavery', drove the point home for me. To be free was to be in the thick of all the buzz and distraction life could offer.

I was a deeply insecure person. I had low self-worth. In the winters, back in London, I would apply for jobs. Then when I got them, I would be so worried about people seeing through me that I wouldn't be able to enter the building. I felt like a human mirage. Empty on the inside. So rather than face the void, I tried to escape it.

The only problem is that you can't run away from yourself. Wherever you go, you're always there. Even on a dance floor at six in the morning.

Running away from yourself is like trying to run away from a lamppost with a bungee cord tied around you. Sooner or later you are going to spring back and have a mighty bump.

Or, in my case, a total breakdown. A full smorgasbord of doom. Panic disorder, depression, OCD, agoraphobia, and a belief that I wouldn't be able to go on living through so much. Which is the irony, of course. My desperate desire to avoid pain and discomfort led to me feeling the worst pain and discomfort of my life. It trapped me inside it. For days, months, years.

And to get out of that I had to ultimately find some kind of acceptance. This might be a funny thing to say in a book with 'comfort' in the title, but pain is a part of life. A part of all life. And so it is also a part of the good stuff too. 'Inspiration and wretchedness complement each other', as Chödrön puts it. But what is good about suffering? What can be *comforting* about suffering? Isn't suffering the opposite of comfort?

At some point, you have to accept your own reality.

Even if that reality includes depression and fear and pain, alongside other things. And when you accept it, you accept other things too. The more genuinely pleasurable things. The pleasure that can be found by being yourself, rather than escaping yourself. Of being able to look someone in the eye, human to human, without any shame or stigma. Of accepting that life connects joy to pain and pain to joy within the same breath.

I didn't need to go out and grab life. I *was* life.

A spinning coin

Uncertainty is the cause of anxiety, but also a solution. While everything is uncertain, everything is hope. Everything is ambiguous. Everything is possible. We exist on a spinning coin. We cannot predict how it will land but we can enjoy the shine as it spins.

You are alive

You can sound confident and have anxiety. You can look healthy and feel terrible. You can speak well in public and be a wreck. You can be externally privileged and not mentally privileged. You can lift barbells and be weak. You can have everything and feel nothing. You can be cut adrift and look ashore.

You are something far deeper than your surface. You are something far deeper than your identity. You are not a value that shifts on a stock market of external opinion. You are part of something bigger. You are part of life. You are part of *all* life. You are an expression of life as much as a dolphin or a lion is an expression of life. You are part of the whole as much as you are an individual. If your individualism manifests itself at the cost of your connection to the whole, you might stumble, but you always have the chance of reconnection. Because life is the way to reconnect with life. And you are alive.

One

Numbers are addictive, because they enable us to measure and compare and quantify while also making us feel there could always be *more*. And numbers – and comparisons – are everywhere. Social media followers. Body measurements. Income brackets. Age. Weight. Online rankings. Click counts. Unit sales. Likes. Shares. Step counts. Sleep counts. Word counts. Test scores. House prices. Budget reports. Stock market valuations. Numbers, numbers, numbers. And the numbers get in. They make us compare. We compare to other people and we compare to ourselves. We don't necessarily do it in a negative way. We might want the best for other people. For our friends and our family. But far too often numbers are involved. I think the numbers get to us. Every value is numerical. We become finite and measurable and of variable value. We lose our sense of infinity. Of life itself. Where numbers exist, measurements exist. And measurements limit us. Because measurements take us from an infinite perspective into a finite perspective. Only finite things can be measured, after all.

One (two)

If you truly feel part of a bigger picture, if you can see yourself in other people and nature, if this *you* becomes something bigger than the individual you, then you never truly depart the world when you die. You exist as long as life exists. Because the life you feel inside you is part of the same life force that exists in every living thing.

Power

The most powerful moment in life is when you decide not to be scared any more.

Growing pains

When everything goes well, we tend not to grow. Because to grow we need to change, because growth *is* change. It is generally when we face hard times that we evolve. Often we need to fail in order to learn, just as a bodybuilder needs weight to resist against. It is impossible to grow in a world without struggle.

Suffering has been stronger than all other teaching, and has taught me to understand what your heart used to be. I have been bent and broken, but – I hope – into a better shape.

Charles Dickens, *Great Expectations*

How to look a demon in the eye

It's easy to want to run away from bad feelings. When we feel sadness or fear we greet them as problems to be instantly solved or dismissed. I can remember that when I was first in the middle of a deep depression, I wasn't just feeling depressed. I was feeling depressed *about* feeling depressed. Anxious *about* feeling anxious. And so, inevitably, the negative feelings kept on multiplying themselves.

The key to recovery lay in acceptance. This was the paradox. To escape depression I had to get to a point where I accepted it. To stop having panic attacks I had to get to a point where I almost *invited* them. I would feel that sudden heightened alertness symptomatic of panic, and I would say to myself *I want this.* This is not a strategy you should necessarily follow. And I certainly don't mean to belittle the horror of a full-blown panic attack. I know as well as anyone how utterly terrifying it can be to feel trapped in your own mind when it is in total freefall. But after a hundred or so panic attacks I realised something about them. They were self-referential. They fuelled themselves. I mean: the panic became worse because I was panicking about the panic. It is a rolling snowball of its own making. But if I stopped myself being frozen *about* the panic, if I melted into a state of acceptance, the panic snowball ended up running out of the ice-cold terror and couldn't grow. Eventually it would float right through. My mind would watch the panic rather than fight it. A totally different type of engagement.

Sometimes, situation permitting, rather than trying to ignore the panic or walk it off, I would just lie down on the floor and close my eyes and really focus on it. And when you really analyse fear you realise, first, that it is only a natural part of us. And second, that it is the sister of hope. Because both are born from the uncertain fabric of life.

In Tibetan the word *re-dok* is a portmanteau of the words *rewa* (hope) and *dokpa* (fear), acknowledging that they coexist and both stem from essentially the same thing – uncertainty. When we analyse rather than evade our darkest fears, we learn that even our largest demons are not as invincible as they first appear. Often, when we stare at them, deeply, they disintegrate before our eyes.

Remember

There will be other days. And other feelings.

Opposites

What would 'big' mean if there was no 'small'? Opposites rely on each other to exist. In Taoist philosophy, the dualistic energies of yin and yang are opposites but also interdependent. Day needs night and night needs day. The dark shadows in a painting by Tintoretto accentuate the light. The mute silence of Maya Angelou's childhood led to her determination to use her voice.

In this world of interdependence opposite emotions are also connected. As William Blake put it, 'Joy and woe are woven fine.' I know this. Because one of the reasons I love life is because I was once suicidal. I have sincerely known more moments of contentment in my life for having gone through years of hell. I now avoid trying to see myself as one thing or the other. I am not a happy person or a sad person. I am not a calm person or a fearful person. I am a happy-sad-calm-fearful person. I let myself feel it all, and that way I am always open to new feelings. Nothing gets clogged in the pipe. No single feeling becomes the *only* feeling, if you let it all happen. And the way to let it all happen is to see the value in it all. To see the way the dark might lead to light. And the way present pain might lead to future hope.

Love/despair

Albert Camus said, 'There is no love of life without despair of life.' When I first came across that quote I thought it was empty and pretentious and more than a little bleak. But as I grew older the words became truer. My love of life stems almost directly from despair. In the sense that I am grateful for better times having known terrible times. But in a deeper sense too. In the sense that pleasure and despair are contained in the same whole, and when we start to see the connections between all things, when we see how opposites are contained within each other, when we see the way everything connects, we can feel more empowered at our lowest points.

Possibility

The existential philosopher Rollo May believed that we often mistake opposites. 'Hate is not the opposite of love,' he said, 'apathy is.' He also pointed out that courage and fear aren't opposites, as fear is an essential component of bravery, and that the truly courageous are those who experience fear and move through it. He was most informative of all, though, when arguing for the compatibility of joy and despair.

'Joy is the experience of possibility,' he wrote, 'the consciousness of one's freedom as one confronts one's destiny. In this sense despair . . . can lead to joy. After despair, the one thing left is possibility.'

The door

Everything in front of us is defined by possibility. We are never inside the future. We are outside the door. We have our hand on the handle. We are turning the handle. But we never know what is on the other side of the door. It may be a room similar to the one we are standing in, or it might be a room we have never seen before. It might not be a room at all. It might be an orchard bearing all the ripe fruits of our labour. It might be wasteland. But we can never be sure. And even if we end up somewhere we don't want to be, we can be thankful for the knowledge that another door exists. And another beautiful handle, waiting to be turned.

The messy miracle of being here

The Western idea of self-empowerment requires you to become better, discover your inner billionaire, get beach-bodied, work, upgrade. It says the present is not enough. It's self-loathing masquerading as salvation.

We need self-acceptance. Self-compassion. Our present bodies and minds and lives are not things we have to escape. We need to remember the messy miracle of being here.

Acceptance

There comes a beautiful point where you have to stop trying to escape yourself or improve yourself and just allow yourself.

Basic nowness

In Buddhism there is the concept of *mettā*, or *maitrī*, meaning benevolence or 'loving-kindness'. *Mettā* is about accepting yourself *as you are*. There is no intent to change you, but rather an acceptance of yourself and all things *as change*.

As Pema Chödrön explains in *When Things Fall Apart*, what makes this concept radical is that there is no attempt to become a better person. It is about 'giving up control altogether and letting concepts and ideals fall apart. This starts with realizing that whatever occurs is neither the beginning nor the end.' Once that happens, you can see that whatever you are feeling is within the normal human range and has been felt by humans since the beginning of our history. 'Thoughts, emotions, moods, and memories come and they go, and basic nowness is always here.'

The concept of *mettā* goes beyond self-compassion,

though. In a *mettā* meditation the aim is to extend compassion first to yourself, then to family and friends, and then beyond that to all beings. Even the difficult ones who annoy us or make us angry. Often this is done via a mantra which begins by focusing on ourselves then moves on to focusing on all of life, spreading out in widening concentric circles of compassion like ripples in a pond.

May I be safe and live happily . . . May she be safe and live happily . . . May they be safe and live happily . . . May all living beings be safe and live happily.

It's beautiful. The idea is that extending compassion to all things helps us to connect to the unity of life. We feel the world's suffering but experience too the joy of life and all nature. We become a part of all things through compassion. We become the metaphorical fire, earth, air and water. We become what we always were. Life itself.

How to be an ocean

You haven't failed,
In a moment of sadness.
You haven't lost,
In a moment of defeat.

You are not a statue
Standing in an eternal contrapposto.
You are a thing in motion:
A rising tide, a cresting wave.

Your vast depths witness
Every marvel, every wonder.
You are, then, marvellous,
And wonderful. So:

Don't fight the moon.
Allow every tide.
And give all your wrecked ships
The space to hide.

More

In troublesome moments, the beauty of life can come into sharper focus. And the things we learn in the bad days serve us in the good times. Just as the promise of good times helps us through the bad. Everything connects. All life is within us. Fear to calm, hope to hopelessness, despair to comfort. A grain of sand can tell us about a universe. And a single moment can teach us about every other moment. We are never only one thing.

Just as our ancestors saw the world as a composite of earth, fire, water and air – so we can see in any moment, in any individual, a connection to all the other elements of that existence. We always have the possibility to be *more*. To be bigger than any current crisis or worry. To discover something new about the landscape of our mind, not by adding to it but by realising it was there all along. The way a page in a book is there even if we haven't read it yet.

We always have more inside us than we realise. More strength, more warmth, more compassion, more resilience.

The world can surprise us, sure, but we can surprise ourselves too.

End

Nothing truly ends.

It changes.

Change is eternal. In being change, you too are eternal. You are here. In this moving moment. And in being here, you are also for ever.

A fire becomes ash, which becomes earth. Sadness becomes joy, sometimes within the same cry. Birds moult feathers, then grow new ones for winter.

Love becomes grief. Grief becomes memory. Wounds become scars.

Doing becomes being. Pain becomes strength. Noon becomes night.

Rain becomes vapour and then rain again. Hope becomes despair then hope again.

A pear ripens, falls, transforms as it is tasted.

A caterpillar disappears into its silk-wrapped cocoon, and things go dark and then . . .

Acknowledgements

Thanks to my agent Clare Conville and all at C+W. And to my editor Francis Bickmore and all at Canongate including Jamie Byng, Jenny Fry, Lucy Zhou, Alice Shortland, Vicki Watson, Vicki Rutherford, Leila Cruickshank, Megan Reid, Caroline Gorham, Rebecca Bonallie, Jessica Neale, Caroline Clarke, Bethany Ferguson, Rafi Romaya, Jo Lord, Katalina Watt, Steph Scott and Drew Hunt.

A massive thank you to all the booksellers for their support over the years, to all the people on social media who have commented on my online ramblings, and to all the readers who have stuck with my writing as I switch back and forth between genres.

And finally, to the wonderful people I live with: Andrea Semple, Pearl Haig, Lucas Haig and Betsy the dog.

Permission credits